W9-BMU-849

PUT ME IN,
COACH

PUT ME IN, COACH

COACH

Confessions of a Football Wife

BARBARA DOOLEY

LONGSTREET PRESS
Atlanta, Georgia

Published by
LONGSTREET PRESS, INC.
2140 Newmarket Parkway
Suite 118
Marietta, Georgia 30067

Copyright © 1991 by Barbara Dooley

All rights reserved. No part of this book may be reproduced in any form or
by any means without the prior written permission of the Publisher,
excepting brief quotes used in connection with reviews, written specifically
for inclusion in a magazine or newspaper.

Printed in the United States of America

Third printing 1992

Library of Congress Catalog Card Number 91-061940

ISBN 1-56352-012-5

This book was printed by R. R. Donnelley & Sons, Harrisonburg, Virginia. The
text was set in Novarese Book by Typo-Repro Service, Inc., Atlanta, Georgia.

Book design by Jill Dible.
Jacket design by Audrey Graham.
Jacket photo by Arthur Usherson.

To my father, who taught me laughter;
to my mother, who taught me love;
to Vincent, who gave me the encouragement to grow;
to Deanna, Daniel, Denise, and Derek,
my ultimate blessings from God.

Table of Contents

"VINCE WHO?"

That was the cry at Georgia in 1963 when they found out that Vince Dooley was their new football coach. I had to laugh when I saw those headlines and heard them whispering. Only a few years earlier I was saying the same thing.

I remember the very first time I met him. I was a student at Auburn and a student in every sense of the word. It was the first time that I had ever been in a Protestant atmosphere (I had been in Catholic schools all my life), and I was away from home with no one in control of my life but me and a very trained conscience. I loved college and everything about it. I loved the cubicle that you call a room, shared by a roommate . . . sometimes two roommates if that quarter happened to be too full. I loved the odds of seven men to every lady. I loved the campus—just being there. I even loved going to class, but of course I would never have admitted that to anyone. One of my most favorite things to do was go to the Student Union between classes and see just who was there to socialize and swap stories with, and it was there that I first met him.

For some reason "the group" had not arrived this particular morning, and I was thumbing through one of my textbooks getting ready for my next class when HE walked up to me and said, "Hi, I'm Vince Dooley." I normally had very good manners and would have said, "Hi, I'm Barbara Meshad," but for some strange reason the way he looked and sounded as he introduced himself made me think he was the most conceited person I had ever met. I must state here that I was not a demure, quiet, humble coed. I had a pretty established ego of my own and a very sarcastic tongue. I immediately looked up at him and said, "So?" I don't remember much else of the conversation, but I do remember telling my friends about this strange "old man" I had met that day by the name of Vince Dooley. One of the football players sitting in the Union building that morning informed me that Vince was a coach there and at one time had been a great athlete. I thought no more about it.

The next Sunday after church I saw Vince approaching, and he asked if I would like to join him for a cup of coffee. Being the polite Southern young lady, I didn't have any reason not to, and I certainly didn't want to hurt his feelings by telling him that he was just too old. So I went for coffee. I wasn't particularly pleasant because I didn't want him even to think about asking me out. After all, I was eighteen and he was twenty-five . . . that was scary! He got the message, and I didn't see him or think about him until the next year when classes started again in the fall of 1958.

It was the first Sunday in October, my second year at Auburn, and as I was leaving church, guess who approached me? It was that coach that I had met in the Student Union last fall. He reintroduced himself and asked if I would like to have dinner with him that night. He caught me completely off guard, and I smiled and said that I would love to. Back during my college years, going out to dinner was really something special, even though it was usually a hamburger and French fries, or at best a hamburger steak with fries—loaded with steak sauce. I asked him where we were going, and he said the Elks Club. I almost died. That was really grown up, a place adults went to . . . not me. Did I know how to act? Did I know exactly what fork and knife to use? "The Elks Club," I told my roommate. "Do you think nice girls go there?"

He picked me up at my dorm with all of my sorority sisters peering out the window to see who this was taking me to the Elks Club for dinner. I didn't know what to order since I had no idea if he could afford anything on the menu, so I played it safe and got the special . . . a hamburger steak!

I guess I didn't act too nice because the end of the evening could not have come too soon for either of us. On the way back to my dorm, he took the back route by the chicken sheds. This was one of the great parking spots on campus, but I was certain in my mind that there was no way this man was going to kiss me good night, let alone park with me. I had a rule anyway that stemmed from my old Catholic high school days that you never let a boy kiss you until the sixth date, and this was only our first (coffee last year didn't count). Plus, I didn't even like him, and I know he didn't like me . . . we just didn't click.

He pulled his white '56 Oldsmobile to a stop, turned off the motor and turned to me. I immediately took the offensive and said, "What do you think you are doing?" He slowly and deliberately rolled down his window and let the odor of the chickens come in, then turned to me and said,

"Do you smell that? Well, that's what you act like . . . chicken shit!" He cranked up his car, rolled up his window, and took me back to the dorm.

That spring I met one of his football players and fell in love. I thought that I was in heaven and that this man was perfect. We dated all that spring, and I stayed and went to summer school and saw him a few weekends during the summer. At the beginning of my junior year I knew that this was the man I was going to marry. Little did I know that Vince Dooley was still in my life.

The first Sunday of October rolled around again, and there he was in church . . . Vince Dooley. I remembered him this time but hadn't seen him since our last date a year ago. He walked up to me after church and we exchanged hello's. He asked me if I was coming to the student meeting at the church that night, and I told him that I was. When I arrived that night at the Neuman Center, I was informed that our new faculty advisor was Vince Dooley. He was handsome, but he was arrogant and conceited, and I was in love with someone else. Plus, I still remembered the chicken shed incident. After the meeting, he asked if I would like to walk with him to get a cup of coffee. I accepted, thinking that this would be the appropriate time to tell him that I was going steady with one of his football players and would probably even marry him. Vince congratulated me and walked me back to my dorm. We shook hands, and I thought no more about it.

A few weeks went by, and Vince began calling my roommate and asking her out. She was dating one of the football heroes of the time, but she liked Vince and began accepting his invitations for Cokes, ice creams, or whatever. Every time he called her, I chided her about that "old man" and told her that she was crazy to jeopardize her relationship with her football hero for a Coke. Vince continued to call her and even asked her to go to church. She was a Baptist and couldn't understand why he would ask her to go to church with him until he asked her to see if Barbara would like to go with them. When she told me that, I knew that Vince Dooley was not out of my life.

I took bowling spring quarter of my junior year, and Vince's coaching friend owned the bowling alley that was downtown in Auburn. Three days a week we had to bowl, and three days a week Vince would just happen to be there. I finally said something to the boy I was going with about Vince hanging around me. He didn't like it one bit and got the courage up one day during spring practice to say to him, "Coach, I would appreciate it if you would leave my girl alone." Vince replied that since we were going steady he would respect that. I felt real bad about this confrontation but relieved that I wouldn't be in an uncomfortable situation again.

I don't want to imply that Vince Dooley did nothing during these college years but chase me. He dated all the time and was engaged twice (though I didn't know all of this until later in the relationship).

The summer of my senior year started out to be perfect. It was my last summer in school, my last year of college. I would be a speech therapist and married to an Air Force officer. I had the world by the tail—until July of that summer. It happened that the boy I was so in love with was not Catholic and had really never understood my roots. My grandparents had come over from Lebanon, and until the day she died at age ninety-four my grandmother still spoke only broken English. That summer, he invited me to spend the weekend with his family in Alex City, Alabama—as I look back on it, to check this girl out. On Sunday, my whole family came to pick me up, including my grandmother. I could tell the minute that everyone got in the living room that our relationship would never work. His family couldn't handle these foreigners, and Catholics to boot. We both knew that it would never be the same between us and that we could never make it together. My family was too important to me. If you can't accept my family, then you can't truly accept me. We broke up.

I went back to Auburn that summer trying to get over this love and trying to finish the quarter and really feeling miserable. One day I was driving down the main street in town and saw Vince in the car next to me. Our windows were rolled down, and he asked how I was doing. I told him not well. He asked if I wanted to talk about it, and I told him okay. I followed him to the country club where he was a member, and as we sat by the swimming pool, I told him what had happened and how miserable I was. He was pleasant and attentive, but he made no move to ask me out. If fact, he didn't even call me after that. I didn't see him again that summer. He knew that he was now in the driver's seat and he would take his time.

At Auburn news traveled fast, and it didn't take me long to get back into circulation and to start going out with lots of different guys. I ended up having a decent summer and was looking forward to home and rest before my last year started.

The first Sunday that we reported back to school, sure enough, there was Vince. We exchanged hello's after Mass and walked to The Grille and had a cup of coffee together. He was fun to see and talk with. We laughed and visited, and he teased me about how fast I "got over" my summertime depression. He asked me out that night for dinner, and I began to see him as a neat person who was a lot of fun. We had a super time that night, and he asked me out for the next weekend. Our relationship flourished, and I fell head over heels in love with him—what an amazing turn-around. We had the same religion and basically the same goals and ideals. He was good looking and from the stories that I had heard had been a wonderful athlete. What more could I ask for? He even belonged to all the clubs in Auburn. Why, he had to be the most eligible bachelor in the world!

We dated every night that fall quarter, and I should have gotten a glimpse of what a disciplined person he was. I was not the student who went to the library on a regular basis; I was there for last-minute papers and exams. But our dates, during the week, consisted of going to the library from seven-thirty to ten o'clock. He was working on his Masters in history. At 10:00 we would walk to town, get a cup of coffee and a dessert, and then walk back to the dorm for curfew (which was eleven o'clock if you were a senior with a B average). This went on every week night. I hated the library, but I endured it just to be with him. My grades did improve, though I constantly disrupted his train of thought with my antics.

When the Christmas holidays arrived that December of 1959, he went home to Birmingham with me to ask my father if we could get married. I thought it was going to be difficult, but he was downright scared.

I was the oldest child of a family of four—and the only girl for sixteen years—and my father had truly spoiled me. Not in the sense that we think of being spoiled, because I remember getting a whipping almost every day until I was a teenager—and Vince contended that I probably needed two a day. But I got most anything I wanted, and Daddy told me daily, before Mother would tell him all the awful things I had done, how wonderful I was . . . how beautiful I was . . . how I was his little girl. No matter how many whippings he had to give me, I was still wonderful! I never lacked confidence nor thought there was anything I couldn't do or achieve if I wanted to.

My dad was a hoot. He loved people, loved to make people laugh, and was generous to a fault. He was the kind of man who never wanted anyone to know that he couldn't afford to have the best. He always drove a Cadillac; that was his idea of having made it. I can remember him coming home one hot July afternoon with perspiration just dripping from his forehead. He was complaining of the heat, and when Mama asked him why all of his windows were rolled up, he answered, "You think I'm gonna let anybody know that I don't have air conditioning?"

So now we were going to ask Daddy if we could get married. Daddy owned a restaurant and seemed to always be there either playing cards in the back room or telling jokes to his regular customers. We went in as usual for a meal and a visit, but Vince was noticeably quieter than normal. I talked twice as much as usual, trying not to let on how nervous we both were, and finally Vince, after he had finished his meal— of course he couldn't ask for my hand on an empty stomach—had the courage to ask the question. My dad was shaken. He looked at us both, slapped his forehead, and said, "All I can say is they've hung the wrong damn Dooley," referring to the then popular song "Hang Down Your Head, Tom Dooley."

We knew that all was going to be okay with Daddy after the news sunk in, so we got the heck out of there—only to find that Vince, in his nervous state, had locked the keys in the car. Vince, at this time in his life, was considered to be quite tight with his money, and his co-workers were always kidding him about his conservative spending habits. The way he took care of his car was a perfect example of this attitude. When we realized that the keys were in the car, I immediately suggested that I tell Daddy and he would help us get in the car. Without one minute's hesitation, he said no thanks and picked up a large rock and broke the side window of his beloved car. He didn't want to look at my dad again that night.

It was our custom during the holidays to have open house on Christmas Day. All of our relatives and friends would drop by, starting from two o'clock in the afternoon and on through the evening. Now let me tell you that being a Lebanese in Birmingham means that you're related to the world, and Vince thought the whole world was in our house that day. He was miserable, and his only solace was a bottle of Scotch and my youngest brother Michael who was ten at the time. They sat in a corner and Vince drank Scotch and played chess with Michael until the last "relative" left. My grandmother never said much, but she watched everything. She was the definite matriarch of the family, still in control of her eight children's lives right up until she died. Grandmother—Siti is what we really called her, which is Lebanese for grandmother—never did accept my father until he died. He had been so wild when he was young—a woman chaser, a gambler, a drinker—and Siti didn't want my mother to marry him. She had a nice doctor picked out for Mother, but, thank heavens, Mother bucked the system and married for love. Daddy never did stop drinking too much, and Siti never did truly open her arms to him . . . until we were saying the rosary over his body at the funeral home and she was crying and saying how wonderful he was.

Everyone wanted to meet this young man who was going to be Wally Meshad's son-in-law, and Vince pulled further and further into his shell and the Scotch. Finally my grandmother called me in the kitchen and said in her very broken English, "That boy you bring home . . . he not Lebanese and he's a sot just like your father." My mother was listening to the conversation and chimed in and said, "I don't care if he's Lebanese or not; the thing that concerns me is that he has shifty eyes." My brothers were not so negative; Vince had duly impressed them by his eating habits. None of us were very big eaters. We just ate because you had do to it. But here was a guy who loved to eat and could eat unbelievable amounts, but, even better than that, he could put a whole chicken leg in his mouth and pull it out clean. Wow, this guy was all right! For years the chicken leg stories went around the dinner table, and our children still don't believe it.

We left Birmingham the day after Christmas and headed for Mobile so he could introduce me to his family, show me his territory, and then we were going to New Orleans to see the Sugar Bowl. I was so excited. This was really living . . . going down to New Orleans—Sin City—with the best looking man in the world. Why, what would the nuns think of this? But Daddy had made it clear that I couldn't go alone with this man, so I asked one of my dearest friends to go with us. She would date Vince's brother Bill and we could room together, which would make all the parents happy.

We had a blast in New Orleans. You could tell he had been there before, but it was all a new experience for me, and he was enjoying showing me everything. We went to a show featuring the Ink Spots, a wonderful vocal group, and it was packed with people waiting to get in. Vince ordered

10

me a Hurricane, the drink made famous in New Orleans. I had never had a drink—that was something that truly turned me off in women—and I drank about a fourth of the Hurricane and got so loud that the vocal group stopped singing and asked me if I wanted to sing. I almost died. Vince never encouraged me to have a drink again, nor did I ever want to.

Winter quarter had started, and so had our wedding plans, but no one who knew Vince ever expected him to go through with this. It was just a matter of when he was going to back out. By this point he had been engaged two times before! One thing was for sure: he wasn't giving me a used engagement ring. When I accepted his proposal, I had three stipulations: I wanted to pick out my own ring, I wanted a maid, and I wanted to be able to go to the beauty shop every week.

In his effort to make sure that he was doing the right thing, he would take me to visit for a weekend with some of his close married friends to see what they thought of me. Each weekend, by Saturday night, the wife would say, "Barbara, you're great, but don't think he's going to go through with this." I never doubted that he would marry me, but just to be safe I had him sleep at our home the night before we got married. I wanted him to know that Daddy was upstairs watching him!

March 19, 1960, finally came, and I walked down the aisle to marry this young coach at Auburn. He was so nervous that his hair was standing straight up, and every time the photographer looked at him, he would say, "Mr. Dooley, please comb your hair." The church was full . . . and his friends were still shaking their heads that he was really going through with this.

Our wedding reception was a typical Lebanese party . . . lots of food, drink, music, and friends. As we were about to leave for our honeymoon, Daddy came up to us and said, "Vince, take care of my little girl." Vince, who is now really brave in front of my father, said, "She's my girl now." Daddy, who had had more than his share of alcohol, ripped off his tux coat and said, "You want to meet me outside and fight about it?" I almost died right there!

Our honeymoon was going to be at the Grand Hotel in Point Clear, Alabama. This was a dream of Vince's. As a young boy growing up in Mobile and working during the summers at camps, he knew that the Grand Hotel was where the rich from the North spent most of the winters and the rich from the South spent their summer vacations. He wanted nothing but the best for our honeymoon. He had saved $200 for this seven-day escape from the world.

On the road to Mobile that afternoon we were both exhausted from the wedding, and we fell asleep in the car. Only when we ran off the road did we realize how worn out we really were. We got to Mobile about dinnertime and stopped at a restaurant on the causeway that he remembered fondly and wanted to share with his new bride. We walk in — I'm still in my going-away suit, hat, and corsage, looking like the last rose of summer — and we meet four of his old girlfriends. They were having a girls' night out, so he asked them to join us. I spent our first evening together as husband and wife listening to high school stories of their fun times in Mobile and eating scallops. I didn't think I liked scallops, but he insisted that I loved them so he ordered them for me anyway. I still hate them! (Vince, still, after thirty years of marriage, orders me what he wants me to eat — so he can have two dinners.)

We spent our first night at Spanish Fort in Mobile and then moved to the Grand Hotel the next day. After two days there Vince decided that we probably should check out because it looked like we couldn't afford it there much longer. It was fifty dollars a night, which included three gourmet meals and all activities. We were the youngest people there by thirty years, and the highlight of the day, for the others, was bowling on the green. We checked out, none too soon, and spent the remainder of the week, and our last seventy-five dollars, at a Holiday Inn at Dauphine Island—for ten dollars a night!

"WHAT CAN YOU DO WITH A GIRL?"

Vincent had rented us a Duplex in Auburn and I thank God that no one lived next door to us. We had a hard time adjusting to married life, and it was best that no one could hear us. This duplex cost fifty dollars a month, and they paid the water; plus, it was furnished. You couldn't beat that, but it was so small that it didn't even have room for doors. The only doors in the place were the front, the back, and the bathroom. It was all we needed, though; I was in school finishing up that senior year, and he was coaching and working on his Masters.

Vince was in the Marines before I met him, and he continued his service by staying in the National Guard, which meant that he had to go to summer camp every summer. So this first summer of our marriage, he was going to take me to Norfolk, Virginia, and then we were going to blow some of his savings and fly to New York from there for a weekend so he could show me the big city. We were so excited we could hardly wait for school to end so we could make the big trip. I had never been to New York, but I was ready to become a twenty-year-old woman of the world.

The day we were to leave, I packed and went to the beauty shop to get ready for our two weeks away. The minute my head went back to get shampooed — I still remember it as if it were yesterday — I became nauseated. We loaded the car, and I grabbed a pillow and got in the back seat, hoping sleep would cure me. Vince was giving a Marine buddy a ride with us to Norfolk to summer camp, and he got in front with Vince. I slept and threw up all the way, with both of us thinking that tomorrow I'd be all well and perky. Vince bought me a bottle of Pepto Bismol because anytime he had indigestion or nausea, that was his cure. I took the first big dose right before we left, thinking I would be fine by the time we got to South Carolina. Then when we got to South Carolina, Vince said, "You've got a really bad case of indigestion. Take some more Pepto Bismol." By the time we got to Virginia, I had taken two full bottles of the pink stuff and was still no better off. But Vince was insistent that Pepto Bismol was the answer — I just had an unusually strong case of indigestion — so he bought a third bottle as we checked into the room in Norfolk.

The next day, as he did every day he was there, Vince got up at 6:00 a.m., put on his Marine clothes, and went out to play war games for the day. At 4:30 he would come back to the room, expecting to see his bride all ready to go to the Officers' Club to party and have dinner. I would open the door, still in my nightgown, hair not combed, no makeup, and run to the bathroom and throw up. "You'll be alright in a day or two. You just have a virus," he would say. All I knew was I was sick and wanted to die.

Sick or no sick, we left for New York as planned, and Vince was so excited to be taking me there. He wanted me to see Times Square, wanted me to eat at Mama Leone's, wanted me to taste Lindy's cheesecake. All I wanted to do was go to bed or die, whichever would come first. Vince couldn't understand what was wrong with me, but he knew that he was going to get me well, and he knew that anytime anything had been wrong with him, Pepto Bismol had been the answer. So that was the answer for me. Three bottles later—and to this day I can hardly type the word—I was still as sick as I could be.

At this young age Vincent had a terrible temper, and when he lost it, you didn't want to be around. Here we were in the middle of Times Square; he had saved his money to give me this treat and to show me around, and all I wanted to do was go to bed. He lost it big time! He was so angry at me that he hit his fist on the dresser so hard that it cracked the glass. I knew that no matter how sick I was, I was going to have to see New York. We went to Mama Leone's. I tried, but I lost it before he even paid the bill. We walked all over New York, and I found every bathroom along the strip. We ended up at Lindy's to get their famous cheesecake, and I just couldn't stand the odor. He insisted that I have just one slice—I couldn't be in New York and not have cheesecake—but I barely got the first bite down. He was furious with me and couldn't understand what was happening. I couldn't either; I just knew that I was green!

We left New York and stopped in Washington on our way back to North Carolina to visit my aunt and uncle. When we walked in and I told her how sick I was, she started laughing. She told me that twenty years ago my mother had walked in her home with the same green look that I had, and nine months later I was born. Vince and I looked at each other, both of us in shock. That had never entered my mind. No one had ever discussed having babies with me, and I thought you had babies when you wanted them . . . not now. I just couldn't be. Vince sent me home for the rest of his summer camp. He couldn't stand any more of this state I was in. Mother took one look at me and confirmed what my aunt had said. I was pregnant. That was awful, but that wasn't all.

Vince had promised one of his sisters that he would educate her son when he reached the college age, so the third week of June I found out I was going to have a baby and I got an eighteen-year-old nephew to live with us until we could get him a place of his own in September. Bud slept on the couch and literally drove me crazy while I was trying to adjust to being married . . . being pregnant . . . learning to cook . . . not to mention studying and trying to finish my wedding thank-you notes.

I stayed nauseated for nine months, but I tried hard just to get through every day. Each morning, I would get up to fix Vince's breakfast—that's what good wives do, isn't it?—but first I would tie a scarf around my nose and mouth. Then, looking like Hop-A-Long Cassidy, I would fry his bacon and his two over-light eggs. The minute I would put them down in front of him, I would run to the bathroom, intentionally leaving the door open, and throw up. One morning, when he had had all he could take—he was basically a very patient man, but I had put him to the ultimate test—with me heaving and him looking at his eggs, he yelled, "The least you could do is shut our one door!"

We bought our first house that summer knowing that we had to have something larger if the baby was really coming. Our first home was tiny but wonderful, and we went about settling in before the football season started. Vince has never been an idle person, and it was certainly evident back then. Coaching in that era was really a two-season job; you coached and recruited in the fall and you had spring practice. Other than that you had lots of free time. Vince never thought of it as free time but as opportune time. I could never understand why he didn't sit around the office with the other coaches and just talk and laugh and maybe play cards. He said that he wanted to make something of himself and that was not the way to do it. He always had a project going, and consequently, so did I. As much as I loved to socialize, he began to show me that other things in life did take priority. We continued to have a lot of fun, but we didn't waste time. That was never to be his style.

Vince traveled those years at Auburn with Coach Joel Eaves, and they got to be very good friends. He used to tell me that Coach Eaves was so thorough at scouting that the only thing he didn't find out was what color underwear the recruits had on. Mrs. Eaves became my friend at Auburn because I would call her with problems since Vince was on the road with her husband. She was always there when I got into a jam and became my mother away from home. The first football game that fall, I was in maternity clothes for the first time and wearing a maternity garter belt that had no directions. It looked like a harness, and I couldn't figure out how to put it on. Vince sure couldn't help, so I just put it on like I thought it should go. It never did feel right, but I didn't know how it was supposed to feel. I got to the game and started telling Wealthy (Mrs. Eaves) about it and she started shaking her head. By the time we stood for the National Anthem, the garter belt had fallen down and my hose and belt were around my feet. I proceeded to take them off right there on the fifty-yard line, and the next day Wealthy came by to give me a lesson in dressing pregnant.

The fall sped by as I spent most of my time either studying — I was to graduate in December, a month before the baby was due — or making maternity clothes. We sure couldn't afford to buy clothes. Vince was gone every weekend scouting and then left after the Alabama-Auburn game for two weeks of recruiting. I couldn't go home because school wasn't out, so it was the first taste that I had of really being alone. I sewed, studied, and cleaned. Now I was not then nor have ever been one that loved housework, but I wanted that house shining for him when he came home after being gone. I don't think that I've ever worked so hard or been so proud of anything. He walked in and saw the house shining and saw my smile of accomplishment . . . and walked over to the thermostat and wiped his finger across it. Two inches of dust! Whoever thought about cleaning a thermostat? He had gotten me. I fell apart. I had worked so hard and thought it was so perfect; he just couldn't resist showing me that I wasn't perfect.

But he loved me and had bought me a surprise, a huge beautiful box with an elegant-looking bow. I knew it was a great present, and it was — my Christmas dress. It was a red brocade maternity suit, absolutely beautiful and must have cost a fortune. One thing about Vince is that he doesn't quibble about the cost of anything. If he wants it and knows he can afford it, he gets it, and boy was I glad that he saw this suit. Little did I know that I would wear it out! I wore that suit with all of my children, though I must say that it didn't look nearly as spectacular with the fourth as it did with the first.

Mothers are special in so many ways, but my mother always had the ability to say exactly what was on her mind without worrying about how it was coming out (my children will all confirm that I have acquired that trait). At any rate, I had just graduated from college and was home for Christmas enjoying the holidays and waiting for the arrival of our first child. Mother, who hadn't said much about the pregnancy the entire time, looked at me and said, "Thank God you've made it through nine months and haven't had that baby yet." It took me a minute to register in my brain what she was saying, but when I did, I flipped out. I couldn't believe for a minute that she had doubted my morality. When she saw how upset I was she said that she never doubted, "but you do know how people are always counting." I never understood, even back then, "people" who counted. I could never even remember someone's wedding date, let alone how many months before their baby was born. I think that must have been a pastime of that generation.

Sunday morning, January 29, 1960, arrived and I woke Vince at five-thirty telling him that I was having pains and that I thought we should go to the hospital. He wasn't so sure but he agreed that we had better go and get checked. We lived in a small house that was built a stone's throw from our neighbors. All the houses on the block were small and everyone knew everyone and everyone's business. Vince has never been one to share information with anyone, and this was not something that he wanted our neighbors to know, especially if it were a false alarm.

Our carport was right next to our neighbors' bedroom window. My orders were to tiptoe to the car—I could hardly walk but I was to tiptoe—and to not shut the car door till we were at the end of the block. No one was to know until we were sure that it was for real. Two hours later we were sent home and told that it would be awhile yet before I would have the baby. They told Vince to take me for a walk, not to give me anything solid to eat, and to come back when the pains were closer together. We snuck back into the house before anyone knew that we had gone and laughed at how we outsmarted them. All the while my pains were about five minutes apart. We got dressed and went to church — pains still five minutes apart. And of course Vince couldn't miss lunch, so we went to our favorite hamburger place and I could only smell the wonderful aromas. I, who had eaten everything that wasn't nailed down for the past few months, now had to pretend that I wasn't hungry and just drink tea and watch him fill up for the coming ordeal. The pains were still five minutes apart. We got home, changed clothes and went for a walk. A couple of times around the house and then the pains started coming. Wow, I knew that I was going to die. Vince didn't hesitate this time; he knew that he had made his dry run and that this was for real. He kept his head. My suitcase was still in the car, but he made sure that he had gathered up all of his books so that he could study while I was having his baby. He didn't know how long this would take and true to his character, he certainly didn't want to waste a minute. What he didn't count on was that a friend of mine, who was in the hospital for something else, spotted him and literally talked his ear off for the next two hours. Not one page did he get to read.

As they took me into the labor room I could hear Vince in the waiting area saying, "Deer hunting, what do you mean?" My doctor was not there, nor could he be found, so his new young partner was going to deliver Vince Dooley's first child. He wasn't happy. I didn't care; just help me get out of the pain was my only concern. This young liberal doctor gave me a "spinal" which enabled me to watch the birth with no pain. Later we were told that this was not a wonderful choice because of what could have happened, but I really didn't care at that point.

Throughout the pregnancy Vincent had never doubted that his first would be a boy. A girl had never entered his mind until she was born. Mother later said that when Vince called and told them of the birth of their first grandchild, he said, "What can you do with a girl?" Let me tell you, folks: he learned. The minute we got that baby home the bond between the two began.

We came home with no preparations for a baby. I look back on it now and still shudder. My mother had lost two babies before I came along and she insisted that it was a mistake to have a nursery, really bad luck. If something were to happen then you would have all of those reminders. It was much easier to get things after the baby was born, so I came home from the hospital with lists for Vince. The first two weeks were a nightmare. Mother came to help and brought my five-year-old sister, who immediately decided that this baby was uprooting her place in both families. I was so sore that I could hardly move and, to top it all off, I couldn't go to the bathroom because I was so constipated. Here we were: Vince, my mother, my little sister, a brand new baby, and me trying to get adjusted in a cracker-box house with nothing for a baby. Vince would make a run to the store with a list only to come home and find another list waiting for him. Mother was trying to teach us how to sterilize bottles, to punch holes in the nipples so the flow would be right, to pin diapers on so they wouldn't slide off in the crib, and generally teach us how to care for this blessing that we had just received that was tearing our life apart. On top of that he had to deal with a wife who couldn't go to the bathroom. The ultimate blow was when I asked him to help me use a suppository. The idea repulsed him so that he walked out and handed me over to mama, saying that he would be back when my problem was solved. He could take no more. Life was getting tense, and we knew it was time for mother to leave when my little sister, Karen, at age five climbed up on her lap after drinking a Coke and asked to be burped!

Life finally settled down, and of course Vince couldn't understand my wasting time and not working on my Master's degree. He was getting his and felt that while I had the opportunity that I should take advantage of it. He would do his course work in the mornings and I could do mine in the evenings. It would take a little longer but at that age time is certainly no factor. I started working on my Master's in Guidance and Counseling and he continued on his in History. Vince, being the disciplined person that he is, had us both on a schedule. I would go to class two nights a week, and on those nights he would take Deanna and go to a friend's house for dinner. I would meet him after class and we would play bridge. The other three nights of the week we studied from seven-thirty till eleven with a break for dessert about ten. It was the only way that I would ever get through graduate school: push, push, and push. I used to try every trick known to woman to distract him from studying but he certainly had more resistance than Adam, or maybe I didn't have what Eve had!

Being married to Vince didn't even start out easy. He had been the college hero and had gone with the campus beauty. They had gone together the whole four years of college and everyone just expected them to marry. It took me at least the first two years of our marriage to convince people that I was not Nancy, his college love. When they realized that he really didn't marry her, they would say, "Oh, she was gorgeous; I can't believe he didn't marry her." The first time that I heard that, I was devastated, but as time went on it became really funny. I knew that one day I would get the last laugh because I was younger than Nancy and the cards couldn't stay stacked against me forever. Time had to take its toll.

I have always been a person who had to have at least eight hours of sleep a night to be at my best, and I think in my youth I might have needed ten. In any event, in those early years with only one child, Vince would let me sleep in the mornings and he would have his special time with Deanna. He would feed her breakfast and visit with her and then get me up before he left for work. When he was out of town, I would put a piece of dry toast in her bed before I went to sleep and that would hold her up till at least eight o'clock in the morning. (Of course, I would have a stroke if my children did that now to any of theirs.)

When Deanna was a year and a half I found out that I was pregnant with number two. We were thrilled and thought that two years apart was perfect and Vince was ready for that boy. But this was a bad pregnancy from the beginning and it's amazing that I carried him as long as I did. I can remember meeting Vince downtown at the bank in Auburn. We were standing in the lobby as he was introducing me to the bank president, and the next thing I knew I was standing in a puddle of blood. Having no idea what to do (back then one didn't talk about such things in public), I just turned my back, left Vince talking to this man, and walked out the door. I went straight to the car where I proceeded to sit on the front floorboard so I wouldn't mess up our seats. It seemed like hours before Vince came to the car. He had no idea where I had gone and just thought that I was rude and had walked away without saying goodbye to the man. He proceeded to make small talk thinking that he was biding time till I came back, never once realizing what had happened.

I had carried the baby about eight months, when suddenly one night while we were in a movie theater, my water broke. Shocked, I leaned over and whispered to Vince what I thought had happened. Auburn was a small village at the time, and there was probably nobody in that theater we didn't know. There was no way we could leave the theater until everyone else had left, or it would be all over town that my water had broken in the movie. So Vince and I decided to wait until the last person had left and then go straight to the hospital. This was the last movie of the night, and we failed to realize how stupid we would look sitting in our seats as everyone filed out. The lights came on, and the theater emptied, and we sat there talking to everyone as they left. Vince would say, "Oh, we're coming; it just takes her awhile to get moving. We're right behind you." We were like the host and hostess of the theater telling everyone good night. I was literally drenched when we finally got up and left.

We left the theater and I took my usual seat—on the floorboard. I went home and called the doctor. . . no pains . . . no baby. . . just wait. I waited seven days, unable to leave the house, leaking my life away. (This was before the days of adult diapers.) Finally on March 12, 1963, Daniel Dooley was born, and Vince Dooley had his boy.

I must say that the first week home with Daniel was traumatic. We had spent hours with Deanna preparing her

25

for her new baby, but I'm not sure that you can actually prepare anyone for a new baby — certainly not a two-year-old. Every time I fed the baby we would urge her to feed her baby doll. That did not satisfy her; she wanted a baby and a bottle like I had. Vince gave up trying to reason with her, took a church key (a beer opener) and slit her doll's mouth so a regular bottle would fit in it. I thought, "Oh great; all I need is for her to see that and try that number on Daniel." The next morning while I was getting breakfast for everyone, and trying to make formula, but not paying attention to Deanna, I heard Daniel let out a bloodcurdling scream. We both ran in to see what had happened and found Deanna standing over the crib with an empty quart bottle; she had poured a quart of cold orange juice on his face saying, "I feed the baby." That was it! That morning Vince boarded up the crib with plywood so Deanna couldn't get near Daniel. We also put a gate on his door and kept it locked at all times. He started out a prisoner in his own home because of a sister who would all her life dominate him. We forgot all of our psychology in dealing with Deanna and went to the old fashioned way of dealing with misbehavior . . . a good spanking. That got her attention and she soon fell in line and took on the role of a loving big sister (as long as everything went her way).

After that one eventful week, Daniel went back to the hospital and I went with him. I had a strep infection, but he had a staph infection that almost took his life. I didn't have to stay long, but Daniel had to be moved to Children's Hospital in Birmingham, Alabama, where he stayed until he was three months old. I stayed with Mama and spent my time visiting Daniel through the isolation window.

He finally got well enough to bring home and I was just getting used to having two babies when I began that ole green feeling once more. I couldn't be . . . I just couldn't be . . . why, my baby was only six months old! I went to the doctor and he confirmed what I had been dreading to face: there would be another little Dooley coming in June. I remember sitting in his office, crying, and stating that there was no way that this could be possible, and I remember him looking out his window saying that only one time in history had there been that "Star In The East." How could this happen to me and what was I going to tell my mother? This would have to be Vince's job. I was taking no responsibility for this pregnancy.

Of course Vince was thrilled that another one was coming; he just wanted to fill up the house. I have always found that so interesting because he was very seldom home to see just how full the house really was. And the noise level was something that still deafens me when I try to recall those early years. The trip home to Birmingham to announce the coming of Number Three was bedlam. Going to Birmingham was beginning to become an event. For the three day trip we needed a van but in the early 60's that was nothing but a dream. We had to take two of everything because Deanna was still a baby, and now Daniel needed the same equipment. Portacrib, bottles, diapers (cloth ones: in the dark ages we didn't have throw-aways), diaper bucket, sterilizer, potty, high chair—you've got the picture—everything baby needed got packed.

Mother and Dad were always thrilled to see us come. At least, that's what I thought. Can you imagine what they were thinking when we unloaded all of this stuff into their spotless, uncluttered home and took their routine and turned it into chaos? But as wonderful grandparents they never let on that we were imposing or driving them crazy. And because Bud was living with us now, we had to bring him with us too. After dinner on Saturday night we were all sitting on the back porch and Vince got the courage to make the big announcement. He looked at his nephew, not at Mother or Dad, and said, "Well, Bud, did we tell you that we're going to have another baby?" For a minute there was dead silence, then Bud answered, "That's great. If it's a boy I'll be an uncle; if it's a girl, I'll be a aunt." We all looked at each other and began laughing. That certainly did break the ice of Mother's glare. But, oh how sick I was, and now I had two to take care of between throwing up and trying to nap. All I could think of was, "This too shall pass."

Football season, 1963: I loved every minute of it! Mother would keep both children on very special weekends if I would take them to Birmingham and then pick them up. This was a two-and-a-half-hour drive back then, so it had to be really special for me to drive that far for a sitter. November of '63 was one of those special weekends and I drove to Birmingham to leave the children. Florida was playing Auburn and we wanted to have the whole weekend to party with friends who would be in town.

In twenty-four hours JFK would be assassinated and our party weekend would turn into mourning for our President. That was an event so important that most Americans who were over ten years old at the time can tell you exactly what they were doing and where they were when the call came through that "the President of the United States is dead."

JFK died and LBJ became President. It was the end of November. Auburn had had a great year in football and was extended an invitation to the Orange Bowl in Miami; Coach Joel Eaves was named Athletic Director at the University of Georgia; Vince was gone recruiting (signing date back then was the first Saturday in December). I mention these things because they were all important events for the ending of a year, but all I could dream of was going to the Orange Bowl. I had never been to Miami, never been to a bowl game as a coach's wife, and had never really been on a big time trip like this was supposed to be. Every thought I had after Thanksgiving went into getting the children to Mother's, and into thinking about clothes for the big trip. We didn't have a lot of money so I had to get started immediately on the sewing machine if I was to have the proper wardrobe that would fit our budget.

I packed the children up and went to Birmingham since Vince was traveling. Mom would help me with the children and I could have a little time to myself to sew and sleep and just be sick with this pregnancy. (Wonder why you never forget how sick this sick really is.)

One early evening the first part of December, I answered the phone at mother's house and it was Frank Broyles, the head coach at Arkansas, looking for Vince. I told him that he was out in North Alabama somewhere, that I really didn't know where, but I would take his name and number and have him call when he called in. People outside of coaching never understood how you could let your husband go off for weeks at a time, never really knowing where he was. He would always call in, but I'm not sure that he really knew where he would be until he was there.

Soon after Coach Broyles called, but before Vincent called—and I really could hardly wait for Vince to call—Coach Eaves called looking for Vince. With my usual honesty, I asked him why everyone was looking for Vince. He said, "Who is everyone?" I told him about the conversation with Coach Broyles, and he said not to tell Vince about that call until he had a chance to talk with him. Confidentially, he said, "I want to offer Vince the head coaching job at Georgia." I could hardly breathe I was so excited, not really for one moment realizing how that phone call was going to change our lives.

When Vince did call I gave him both messages and told him exactly what Coach Eaves had in mind. He returned his call and then called me to discuss what Joel had offered. It really didn't matter what he had offered: Vince Dooley knew that this was his big break and that he was going to take it. He called me and told me that Coach Eaves had indeed offered him the Georgia job with a starting salary of $12,500, plus a $2,000 subsistence for entertaining and extras that we would have to do. He asked me what I thought, and I remember saying, "Take it, take it, we're rich! This is great, but can you tell him we don't want it till after the Orange Bowl?"

"I can't tell him that," Vince answered. "I've got to take it now and begin work immediately for the University of Georgia, but I promise you that one day I'll take you to the Orange Bowl as the head coach's wife."

"Oh, Vincent," I gushed, "I'm so thrilled for you. I promise that whatever it takes I'm with you and I'll never complain."

Why in the world I uttered those words in the heat of emotion I'll never know, but in a few short months they came back to haunt me.

"YOU CAN TAKE THOSE CARATS AND . . ."

Vince Dooley was all over the papers as the new young mentor at the University of Georgia. His life changed overnight, but mine was still the same. In the midst of the congratulations and confusion, I was still changing diapers, making formula, watching children, and constantly throwing up with number three! He was on a constant high that I couldn't understand because I was not in his world of adulation. Frankly, my life was boring.

How many hours is it to Athens, Georgia, from Auburn, Alabama, with two children, a pregnant wife and a dog? At least an eternity. We arrived in Athens December 30, 1964, and checked into the Holiday Inn. I had five days to find a place to live or go back to Birmingham and stay with Mama. That first night after we checked in, it was cold and raining, and our phone never stopped ringing and Vince never stopped talking. During the night it began to snow, and all of the electricity went out. There we were in a hotel room — two babies and not one watt of electricity — and all of my friends were in Miami enjoying the Orange Bowl. I began crying and wondering what part of the planet earth my husband had brought me to. I remembered promising for better or worse . . . but Athens, Georgia?

When Daniel needed to be fed, Vince would have to leave the room and go to the hotel kitchen where they had an auxiliary unit to heat the bottle. Finally I was so miserable that he could stand it no longer. I dressed Deanna, and Vince took her to the dining room for breakfast, leaving me for about two hours with only Daniel and my miserable attitude watching the Orange Bowl Parade on television and crying buckets of tears.

It was New Year's Eve, and I knew that anything from this point on had to be uphill. Ruth and Bill Hartman, who would become two of our dearest friends, called and invited us to the Athens Country Club for the New Year's celebration. Of course, we didn't go. My idea of celebration was to be left alone to get out of this town. How far away was Miami anyway?

Athens in 1964 was certainly not a booming town as far as apartments went. When we began looking on January 1, there were actually only three apartment complexes available for rent, and they were all full. That seems inconceivable today because we now have apartments coming out of apartments. Just when I was about to pack my bags and go home to Mama, Vince found a furnished apartment with no lease that was perfect for us until we could find a home.

The first year that we were in Athens was something I look back on and shudder. Vince was only home fifty-four nights that whole year. He covered the state so that he could get to know the people and they could in turn get to know him. I broke my promise to him of never complaining, and all I ever seemed to do was cry and feel sorry for myself. I was lonesome, I was scared, I was pregnant, and I wanted my husband. It was many years later that I realized that for $12,500 they had bought, totally and completely, the man I loved. He was going to succeed, and he was going to do whatever it took to do it. I was in such a small world that I'm not really sure I ever felt the magnitude of his job until his last few years of coaching.

The second week of January we moved into what was to be our home for the next few months. It was a two-bedroom apartment, sparsely furnished, and with absolutely no charm. The man who built them had taken out a loan for housing for the elderly and then somehow, right before finishing them, had opened them up to anyone. Anyway, they were perfect for pregnant women and little children. There were pull up rails next to the toilet and on the side of the tub. There were no stairs and all the floors were tile which was easy to clean, but, oh, so cold for little children to play on in January, February, and March. But I decided this was better than going home. At least I would be able to see Vincent and be a part of his new life in Athens. Boy, was I wrong. The only time we saw him was when he was packing to go somewhere else or dropping off dirty clothes. I fussed and I fumed. I certainly had not bargained for this, but I'm a survivor, and I was hanging tough at least until I could find a house and have this baby. Then I knew everything would be fine.

In April we moved into a grand house—at least at the time I thought it was grand. It was certainly more wonderful than anything we had had up to this point, and after a few months in that apartment, the house looked like a castle. Things were looking up. This house had four bedrooms, two and a half baths, two dens, a living room and dining room, a kitchen, and a screened-in porch. I thought

I had died and gone to heaven. Plus, it was two stories and I loved that idea. It certainly didn't take us long to move in. We had one bedroom suite, two cribs, a playpen, some toys, a kitchen table with four chairs, a sofa, two chairs, an ottoman, and two lamps. I'm not sure that we even filled half a truck. We were probably the cheapest move that the athletic department has ever had. We had so many empty rooms that the children could run wild and never hurt a thing. The house was not centrally air-conditioned. There was only one unit and that was in the master bedroom upstairs. Needless to say, in May, my eighth month, we stayed upstairs all day just to keep cool.

I was determined that Vince should be in town when our third child was born, but I knew that I would have to be lucky for that to happen. Denise was due on June 21, which was Father's Day in 1964, and I prayed that she would be right on the day so he would be home. Vince came home about nine o'clock Saturday evening, June 20, and brought Coach John Donaldson, who had been traveling with him. We sat out in the back yard and ate watermelon and talked about what they had been doing all week. John left about eleven, and I knew at three in the morning that the baby was going to be right on time. At six the children got up and we dressed them and put them in the car, and Vince took me to the hospital. He dropped me off and I checked myself in because he now had to baby-sit until he could get some help. He called my mother in Birmingham and said please come as soon as you can. He then proceeded to take both children out to breakfast. You must understand that here is a man who has never changed a diaper, has never kept the two children together by himself, taking them out to breakfast. You must imagine, too, that this is before McDonald's or Hardee's or any other fast food breakfast place. So he took them to the only cafeteria in Athens that opened that early, Davis House. There he proceeded to take a three-year-old and a fifteen-month-old through the line, asking them what they would like. By the time he got them to the table, Deanna had knocked over the orange juice and Daniel had rubbed egg in his hair. He finally got Daniel into his high chair and Deanna in her booster when Daniel knocked over his milk. He couldn't get out of there fast enough, and he was so embarrassed that I'm not sure he ever returned.

It's only nine in the morning by now. Vince knows that it's a four-and-a-half-hour drive from Birmingham, and he could only hope that Mother had left when he called her. He had a long morning ahead of him. The heat on June 21 that year broke all records, and the morning had started out hot and sticky. Vince turned on the one air conditioner upstairs, took a cup of coffee and the paper, and sat on the floor to read while they played. All was going well until he began to smell an odor. He knew immediately it was Daniel and he was going to have to change his first-ever diaper. But how? What do I do? This has got to be awful! He took the diaper off, threw it in the toilet, took Daniel and Deanna outside, and hosed Daniel off. Then he filled the plastic pool with water and put his bathing suit on. Mother said when she arrived he was sitting in the pool with a child on each side and holding a hose over their heads. They were clean and cool. When he arrived at the hospital, he sent me a message that baby-sitting was a piece of cake.

Denise was born that afternoon and was without a doubt the best Father's Day present that I have ever given him. We now had three children, a new job, and I had to begin to adjust to this new life.

Three children under three was a handful, and all of my new friends kept telling me what a wonderful family three was, but I knew that we weren't finished. Vince Dooley wanted another boy, and I was certain that I wouldn't stop until we got him. But please, Lord, give me a little break. I did have a little break. Derek wasn't born for four years, June of 1968. As usual for me, I was sick from the time of conception until I delivered. And this fourth one was no different. The difference with this one was that I had a little household help, a wonderful baby-sitter, and some fantastic friends. So things didn't seem nearly as terrible as they had during the first three pregnancies. Vince was still gone all the time and I was still bitching about his never being home and about never having a social life and about life in general, but things were getting better. Then I got a call in December and Vince said, "Barbara, you know this baby you're having?"

"Yes," I said.

"Well, when did the doctor say it was due?"

I paused. I knew something was coming that I wasn't ready for. "The last date he gave me was June 10."

"Do you really think it's gonna come on that date?"

"Well, Vincent, how do I know when it's really going to come? It can come two weeks before that or two weeks late. All I know is that Deanna came on her due date and so did Denise. Why?"

"Well, I have this opportunity to do a coaching clinic in the State of Washington from June 10 through June 13, and it would be some extra money, and I'd like to see that part of the country."

I went silent for a moment. I knew that if I said not to go he would definitely go. We both have that kind of personality: to tell us not to do something is like backing us up against a wall. So very bravely I answered, "Just go on and go; it probably won't come on that very day."

The spring Southeastern Conference meeting is usually held the last weekend in May, and of course Vince had to be there. I was hoping that our fourth would come early, as had Daniel, so that Vince would feel comfortable about going to Seattle in June. He called every afternoon from the SEC meeting, and all I could do was laugh because he asked the same question each day: "When do you think it's gonna come?" He was praying it would be before the ninth because he really wanted to be home for the birth, but he had made a commitment that he could not back out on at this late date. And I should add that we did need the extra money. As June 9 approached and my state was still unchanged, he volunteered to cancel his trip. I, still trying to be brave, said, "Oh, go. This baby might be another two weeks away. Who knows?"

Never once did I really believe that he would go. From that experience I learned never to play games with someone, especially your spouse. Tell him straight up how you feel. He had made a commitment, and I might have known that on June 10 he would walk out the door for Washington. What I didn't know was that he had promised Coach Erk Russell, his head defensive coordinator, that he would go with him to Las Vegas after the clinic and would not return to Athens until June 16.

Vince did indeed leave on June 9, and Derek did indeed arrive on June 10, and it was indeed a day that I will never forget. It was a Monday, a hot, sticky Monday, and I had spent the whole day at the club pool entertaining the children. I began cramping that afternoon when we got home, so I fed the children, bathed them, and got them ready for bed, and I called Linda, my faithful baby-sitter, and told her to come and bring her pajamas since I might be going to the hospital. Then I called our dearest friends, the Chilivises, who had been checking on me daily to see if I needed anything, to take me to the hospital. No answer. Then I called my friend and closest neighbor, Bobbie McDonald, and told her that I thought I was in labor. It's strange how even with the fourth baby, I was not sure I was really in labor. She had six children and she came right over, took one look at me, and knew that I was in serious labor. She called my doctor and took me to the hospital. Again, I was dropped off. I was hurting too much to check in, so I went straight to the delivery room. There my wonderful doctor, Bill Crosby, was waiting for me. He knew I was scared. He knew Vince was gone, and he did everything that he could to make this wonderful event truly wonderful.

When I woke up hours later, he was sitting at my side. The hospital had not been able to reach Vince because of the time difference, but it was now three in the morning — midnight where Vince was — and Dr. Crosby tried to reach him for me. Vince answered the phone, and I said, very weakly, "Vincent, I just had the baby and it's a boy."

After a second of stunned silence, Vince said, "A boy . . . well, I'll be damned."

I told him how much he weighed and how long he was, and Vince said again, "Well, I'll be damned." Then he hung up. Two minutes later the phone in my room rang. It was Vince.

"Barbara, are you sure it's a boy?"

"Vincent, I'm positive."

"Have you seen him?"

"Yes, he just left the room."

The next thing I heard was a click . . . he just hung up. The man was out of his mind over his new boy.

The next day, after a good night's sleep, he called and carried on a normal conversation with me, and we began discussing names. Since we already had three that began with "D," this one had to have a "D" name too. My choices were Derek and Darrell. He said that he had to go to a meeting but would call me back and let me know what he thought the better of the two would be. Little did I know that he was going to ask two hundred coaches to vote on the name that they liked the best. Derek won.

Now wouldn't you think that after giving your husband the second boy he wanted he would rush right home to be at your side? Wrong. He had made a commitment to go to Las Vegas, and he was going. He would be home as planned. I decided that he could go anywhere he wanted to, but I was not checking myself out of the hospital. I had checked myself in, but he was checking me out. So I stayed. And each day the good sisters at St. Mary's Hospital would come by and say, "Are you going home today?" and I would say, "No, Sister, not today." People in town began feeling sorry for me and bringing me food—platters of food—and I ate everything they brought. I'm probably the only patient in history who weighed more when checking out after delivering a baby than when checking in. Finally, six days after Derek was born, Vincent came to the hospital and took us home.

He felt so guilty about not being with me and taking so long to get home that he had with him a two-carat diamond ring as my gift . . . and then he had the nerve to bargain with me.

"For every baby you have from now on, I'll upgrade you a carat."

I told him that I was happy with what I had and he could take the other carats and sit on them! That's not really what I said but I don't want my mother to think I talk ugly.

ATHLETE I AM NOT

I was a Toy Bowl cheerleader in grammar school, and that was just about the extent of my athletic endeavors until I met Vince Dooley. Physical Education courses were fun, but those that didn't make me sweat or expose me to the elements were my favorites. Those criteria left bowling as my favorite PE class at Auburn. I was fairly good. I could keep my makeup intact, wear cute clothes, and smell fresh even when it was over.

I've never liked the smell of sweat, and to me that was the mark of an athlete—odor! I remember when my children were young and would come in from playing on hot days their smell would almost nauseate me. And several sweaty boys in a carpool would just about put me away. I'd drive with the windows open and my nose to the back of my hand where I had sprayed perfume. The minute I got home, I would spray my car with a deodorizer so it wouldn't have that locker room smell.

Vince has always said that I was the only girl he didn't date a full year just to check out her athletic ability, and he married me without knowing my history in this area. He is the ultimate competitor. If he is behind in whatever game he might be playing, he will dig deep into his guts to find a way to beat you. And when it comes to playing with the children, he's not above cheating to win. I've seen them come in from a basketball game with the children screaming, "He cheat. We had him beat, and he cheated and won!" Vince would taunt them by saying, "You just think I cheated. The best man won."

I don't have this attitude toward sports. My thoughts are, "It's only a game, and the sooner we get it over with the sooner we can socialize."

Never having been in really competitive sports, I never learned how to get a winning mind-set. This is part of my personality that would drive Vince crazy. He always understood that developing a winning mind-set is half the battle, and that without it you're lost. Through the years, no matter how hard I tried, no matter what the sport, I couldn't match up, and he had little or no patience with me.

Our first experience together as a team came shortly after our first child was born when we became friends with another couple on the Auburn coaching staff. They were into playing bridge and invited us to play with them. I had played all through college but very socially. Deal a little, talk a lot. We had so much fun the first night that they invited us back, and it became our constant entertainment. One great thing about it was we didn't have to get a baby sitter. Who could afford fifty cents an hour to play cards, or to play anything?

How well I remember our first real vacation. We met Vince's brother at the Gulf, and what a week that turned out to be. Bill's wife was no more of an athlete than I was, and he was just as competitive as Vince, so we were evenly matched for whatever we were going to do. Before we could even unpack, Vince and Bill had rented a small boat so that we could go fishing. It sounded like fun until the reality set in. There was live bait in that boat that Vince assumed I would touch. Why, he even thought I would bait my own hook. I looked at it, and then I looked at him; I just couldn't do it. There was no way that I could touch those creatures.

I had grown up in Birmingham, and I had only been fishing one time in my life. I sure had never touched anything like live bait, or even a dead fish. So now I decided I didn't want to fish; I just wanted to sit in the boat and get a suntan. Well, Vince didn't like that attitude. I was a quitter, and he couldn't stand that. He loved to fish and just couldn't understand where my mind was. It didn't take him long to catch a fish, and as he brought it in, I jumped and screamed because it was flapping all over the boat and I didn't want it to touch me.

I could tell that he was losing patience with me. I was not getting into the swing of the party, and he said in a stern voice, "One more negative and you're going into the water." Well, there was no way he was getting the last word with me, so I made a smart comeback. Now Vince has always been a man of his word, and within thirty seconds, with a look of ultimate devilment on his face, he had lifted me up and thrown me out of the boat. I started hollering and carrying on in a way that he had never seen. I was disrupting this quiet lake, as well as the other fishermen, but I was going to scream until he let me back in the boat.

This did nothing but frustrate him. He could not believe that I was afraid of fish, and dead fish at that. He got completely frazzled and knew he had to get me back in the boat.

So, without thinking, in an effort to get me back in and calmed down, he decided to get rid of the fish. He picked up the cooler and dumped the few fish he had caught overboard. He didn't realize just exactly what he had done until I went into orbit. Here I was, treading water, and dead fish were floating around the boat. His face took on a look of horror, as did Bill's and Chris's, when he realized his good intentions had turned on him. That was one time I prayed to walk on water, and although my prayer wasn't answered, Vince told me after they caught up with me and pulled me back in that I had broken the Olympic record for free-style swimming.

I knew that I never, ever, wanted to go fishing with Vince again, and it was years before I ever even got in a boat with him again.

They fished most of the week, and Chris, Bill's wife, and I were bored. She was a fair-skinned blonde, and I was a dark-skinned brunette. Total opposites. The last day of our trip the men went fishing, and Chris decided to bleach her hair. Of course, out of boredom, I decided I wanted her to bleach my hair, too. I would surprise Vince with the new me! I've never thought of myself as a beauty, but back in my youth I did have pretty hair — very dark, thick, and lots of natural curl. That all ended with the bottle of bleach. My hair turned bright orange, and with my suntanned skin I looked like a two-bit hooker.

I tried to laugh, but I knew that when Vince saw me he would flip. At first he thought it was a joke, but as the evening wore on and he realized that what I had done was for real, he became totally silent and would have nothing to do with me. The next day we went to church in his home town of Mobile, and he wouldn't even sit with me. He said he didn't want to be near anything that floozy-looking in the world. That Sunday evening we went by a drugstore and got some brown dye to cover the orange. It helped the color but ruined by hair. I'm just thankful that thirty years later I still have hair.

Shortly after coming to Georgia, Vince had met a young lawyer named Nick Chilivis, and they became instant friends. He was single, good looking, intelligent, and loved to play bridge. He was dating Patti Tumlin, one of the Georgia cheerleaders, and we were thrilled when they decided to get married. Not long after the marriage, we began weekly bridge games that were fun until we began playing for money. We decided to keep the winnings in a pot so that after a few years we would have vacation money for the four of us to go somewhere. Sounded like fun to me, except I seemed to always be on the losing team.

At first it was funny, but then it began to be a thorn in our marriage. We would go home at night not speaking to each other because of some dumb bridge hand. The madder he got at me during the game, the more uptight I would get, and the worse I would do. Finally we set a rule that we would start out with our spouses but could never end up with them, hoping that that would reduce the tension. But that didn't work either. I would start Vince's night off badly, and that would set the tone for the night. The most vivid recollection I have of war at the bridge table was on a boat in Hawaii. Nick and I were partners, and I bid seven no-trump. We had absolutely everything but one ace, and I knew that Patti had it but Vince would have to lead to her.

If he doesn't lead right, we make it; if he does, we're down. We're vulnerable and doubled, so it's a huge hand.

As Vince is thinking what to lead, Patti says, "Vince, lead 'em right." Well, he did, and they set us by seven tricks which cost us a zillion points! I went berserk and accused them of cheating by talking across the table, and Vince just kept rubbing it in. Our bridge games became nightmares for me, and finally one night after Vince kidded me once too often, I vowed never to deal the cards with him again. I don't think anyone took me seriously, but that was really the end of our bridge games. Perhaps we'll play again after our Golden Jubilee, but in the meantime how about another "togetherness sport"?

Tennis anyone? Maybe we could play mixed doubles. Tennis became the rage in the seventies, and I was right in the middle of it. I took lessons, bought all the right clothes, and had the best equipment, but I played only an okay game. I was never quick enough or fast enough to be an "A" player, but I was at the top of the "B" players. I thought I was good enough to be Vince's partner — until we tried it together. The name of the game with him was win. With me it was fun. His theory was you have fun after you win.

Playing together just didn't work. Vince would constantly tell me what to do, poach on my side of the court, and then if he missed the shot it was my ball. So we decided to split up and play against each other. How did that work? Not much better. Most men would have the courtesy not to hit the hardest ball they could to their wives, or if it was match point not to aim straight at her, or glare at her across the net and say, "I'm coming at you next shot." Vince loved to stir my emotions, and he knew how to push my hot button. He wanted to win, and he knew that he could psyche me out totally by a hard ball or even by a look, and he took full advantage of my athletic shortcomings.

One afternoon when we were playing with another couple, on match point he looked across the net in his cocky way and said, "Watch out. I'm coming at you." And he did. He slammed in right on my feet. I got so mad I threw down my racket and jumped over the net ready to attack, and he just laughed and started to run. We broke up about five tennis games during the chase, but I knew I was through with tennis! That was it. I wasn't going to do anything that would put an extra burden on our marriage. Marriage to Vince was hard enough as it was.

I grew up in Birmingham, and we never really had access to boats and water. Vince grew up in Mobile and loved everything about the water. He grew up part fish. Water skiing was a sport that I had heard about but had never had an opportunity to learn. Coach Donaldson, who was from Jesup and on our first staff, had a boat and loved to take it to the lake and ski. He and his wife, Ann, asked us to go one weekend, and it sounded like fun so we went. Ann skied. Vince skied, and I was shocked at how good he was. John skied. Now the time had come for me to give it a try.

Anyone who has ever learned to ski has heard the same old advice: "You don't have to do a thing. Just let the boat pull you up." That boat never did pull me up. I must have fallen thirty times, and each time John was there to reassure me that my fall was not as bad or as quick as the previous one, that I was getting better. Finally, I got to the squatting position and went around the lake with Vince yelling, "Stand up!" But I just didn't have the guts to stand. About two months later I managed to stand, and we all declared that John was the greatest coach in the world. Nothing athletic was natural for me.

I don't know when Vince decided that we needed to get into snow skiing, but I certainly can remember the first time we went. We went with his old teammate from Auburn, Fob James, and his wife, Bobbi, who is about as athletically inclined as I am. Fob has a house in Toronto, Canada, and the slopes were not far from there. None of us had ever tried it before, so we were all wild with anticipation. The learning slope was very steep and had a rope-pull to take you to the top. Staying on the rope with a disc seat between your legs was almost as challenging as getting down the mountain.

First of all, my boots were a size too small, and after an hour of trying to learn with a Canadian instructor, I had absolutely no feeling in my feet but pain. All I wanted to do was get those boots off and fast. I went to the lodge, returned the boots, and watched Vince and Fob the rest of the day. As usual Vince caught on fast and was coming down the slopes with ease. It didn't take long for his confidence to grow into cockiness, and I started praying for a humiliating spill. It didn't take long for my prayers to be answered. Vince was going up the tow-rope when somehow his skis got tangled and he went head-first into a ten-foot snowbank. All you could see were his skis coming out of the white mound. I needed a good laugh after my own failure, and he sure gave me one.

There's a sense of adventure in Vince. It seems that there's nothing he doesn't want to try. He is proud that he flew an F-16 Fighter at Moody Air Force Base in Valdosta and went soaring over Pike's Peak in a glider at the Air Force Academy. Scuba diving was to be his next area of excitement. After he took diving lessons, which I was totally opposed to, he began trying to get me to take lessons. I took a couple of lessons to please him, but I truly hated every minute of it. First of all, I've never trusted myself in a panic situation, and what would I do if something happened sixty feet below water that I couldn't predict? I've never been drawn to animals, except dogs, so why did I want to swim with fish? And finally, it was an eerie feeling to me to hear no sounds except the breathing from my tank.

Well, we got invited to go to Bimini for a long weekend of diving, and Vince was just beside himself. It was clear from the start that I wouldn't have to dive if I didn't want to. I could just enjoy the boat, the weather, the company, and all the fresh lobster they were going to catch. It sounded like fun to me but a real adventure to Vince. They were going to go spear-fishing, which he had never done before. There were ten couples, and two of the guys were former football players of Vince's: Bill Cole, a professional diver, and his good friend, Mack Guest, who was an All-SEC tackle on Vince's '78 WonderDog Team.

For three days I watched the group make two and sometimes three dives a day. After each dive they would exclaim that was the greatest dive they'd ever had. It was almost a joke to witness the euphoria as they ascended from the deep. I was delighted that they were having such fun, but I never once wished to join them. I knew it was coming, though, when after the second day Vince casually mentioned that I ought to go down for a short dive. Our professional would be with me, and it would be fun. I said no. Undaunted, as he usually is when he's got something on his mind, he kept after me. (I've often told him that if he were a woman he'd be labeled a nag because he won't get off of your back until you do what he wants you to.)

Sure enough, on the last day, and totally against my wishes, he announced to Bill that I was going to dive, and I knew that I didn't have a choice. Praying for a whale to eat me up just to prove to Vince that he shouldn't have made me, I went down about fifty feet. I was sucking oxygen so fast that I ran out of an hour's supply in thirty minutes. I saw a sand shark below me and an eel straight ahead looking at me, and I clutched Bill's arm with all my strength. If they got me, they were going to get him too. Finally, we surfaced.

"Now wasn't that wonderful?" beamed Vince.

I wanted to say, "Hell no," but I restrained myself and said, "Yes, it was the most wonderful thing I have ever done, but I don't ever want to do it again."

"Why not?" he asked.

"Because, Vince," I explained, "you can't talk, and I hate being quiet that long."

It was such a logical and truthful statement coming from me that he accepted it, and I've never had to go under again.

So much for sports!

"Play Me or Trade Me!"

Shopping has always been a part of my nature and nothing makes for a greater day than finding a bargain, or even not finding a bargain. Shopping is the ultimate! Most men don't understand a woman's need in this area, and they certainly get no thrill from a bargain. A man's point of view is directly opposite to the woman's: the more it costs, the better it must be. Plus, I don't think most men have the patience to really shop for an item. If they want something, they want it right then, and they buy it. Heaven forbid you take them with you on a shopping trip. An hour's tolerance is the max; after that, you both are growling. He doesn't like the way you shop, and you don't like the way he makes you nervous. I have always wondered about couples that shop together.

The first hint I had that Vince was not a shopper was during our engagement period. We went to downtown Birmingham with my mother to pick out our china and silver patterns. This is certainly a monumental moment in an engaged couple's life. My mother, however, has never been known for her tact or for holding anything in, and, right in front of the salesperson, she proceeded to comment on how tacky a certain pattern of china was. That completely undid Vincent, that someone would talk so openly in front of a salesperson. So our first shopping encounter with each other became our last for years to come. In fact, the only other times that I can remember his shopping with me were on trips out of the country, and even then he would only concede to an hour.

Aren't the early years of marriage wonderful? Thoughtfulness abounds each and every day. The first four years that we were married he bought me a little something almost every time he went out of town. And he complained about how my daddy had spoiled me! I can still remember the first time he went to Chicago and came home with two silk scarves from Marshall Fields. Well, I had never even heard of Marshall Fields and was so impressed by my cosmopolitan husband. I still have those two scarves today and look upon them with such fond memories. Little things can mean so much when you're young, poor and madly in love.

After Denise was born in June 1964 and we had gotten home and settled in, Vince came walking through the door with a large box tied with a beautiful ribbon. I knew it was for me and could not wait to see what I was getting for birthing this baby girl. With adolescent eagerness, I ripped open the package, and there in front of me was a leopard-skin bathing suit with one shoulder. Here I was fifteen pounds overweight after just having produced the child of his loins, and I am being presented with a sexy bathing suit that my cellulite would never fit into again. I know that I looked shocked, but I tried to control myself and just prayed that it wouldn't even begin to fit so I would have a reason to take it back.

I wanted to handle this moment with great aplomb. My dad always gave my mother money for special occasions because in the early days of their marriage she always returned everything he gave her. I didn't want that to happen to me, but I also didn't want an off-the-shoulder bathing suit. I mean, really now, could you imagine my child-bearing body at the Country Club baby pool in a one-shoulder leopard-skin bathing suit? I need not have worried. I couldn't get one thigh into it and happily meditated on my good fortune as I munched one more Little Debbie cake before taking it back.

Another story that comes to mind took place when we were still in Auburn, after Deanna was born in January of 1961. Mother's Day came, and I was anxious to celebrate my first Mother's Day as a real mother. The morning came and went, and nothing. Finally, at lunch, I began crying and telling Vince how I couldn't believe that he had forgotten Mother's Day. He looked shocked and said, "You're not my mother." I retorted, "I'm sure not, nor would I ever want to be, but I am your child's mother!"

Later on that afternoon he drove to the drug store — the only store that was open on Sundays back in the dark ages — and bought me a book by Dr. Spock and a hair brush. He came home all full of himself and gave me the presents with his devilish grin. I think I threw the brush at him, but Dr. Spock did get us through all four children.

How can anyone forget Christmas? Well, my husband did. In 1967, he was asked to coach the Blue-Gray game in Montgomery, Alabama, on Christmas Day, and he accepted. He thought this would be a good idea since we always went to my home in Birmingham for Christmas, and

Montgomery is close to Birmingham. He spent the entire Christmas week in Montgomery, driving into Birmingham only once, and then he was to come back to Birmingham on Christmas Eve. Our family always has the big Christmas dinner on Christmas Eve, and then we all sit around and open presents. Vince was due in early that evening to have dinner, open presents, see Santa Claus, and then leave early the next morning to be back in time for the big game. On the way to Birmingham, however, he realized that he had bought nothing for me nor anyone in my family. Never one to panic, he pulled over at a Stuckey's and proceeded to do his Christmas shopping. Everything that Stuckey's sold he brought to Birmingham. He was always a stickler about my picking up his mirror in the bathroom, so he decided to buy me my own hand mirror. He bought six — one of every size they had. Each was wrapped separately, and in the smallest mirror there was a $100 bill. Back then that was like getting $1,000, but I didn't want money for my present. Once again he had come through in the fourth quarter, and victory was on his face. I've always wondered what the salesperson at Stuckey's thought about a man buying six mirrors and eighteen boxes of assorted candies.

Christmas seemed to be the hardest holiday for Vince to remember because he was either recruiting or in bowl preparation during that month and the days just slipped by. I have always loved clothes and loved different kinds of clothes, but this particular Christmas when I opened the box I knew that this dress was not for me. I also knew that some salesperson had really done a number on him; Vince is such a softie with salespeople. You must get the picture: I had four little children, and the only places I went to regularly were church and the grocery store. If I went out at night it was usually casual, so you can understand my dismay when I opened the big package wrapped in gold ribbon from one of the nicest shops in Athens, and there before my eyes, nestled in a dozen layers of tissue, is a size 12 (I don't think I've ever been a size 12) red velvet dress with white fox trim around the hem. I thought to myself, "What does this man think I do all day and night when he's not here?" But I gathered my composure, told him how much I loved it, and proceeded to try it on, knowing full well that it would droop all over me and I would have a legitimate reason for exchanging it. Did it ever droop.

As Vince was looking at me in the dress, I noticed a strange look cross his face just for an instant, but I dismissed it as my imagination and thought no more about it. I was to learn that my intuition was on target because I took the dress back to the store the next day and the lady who sold it to Vince came up to me. I explained that the dress was lovely but it was too large, and could I please exchange it for something else. I said, "Could you show me some other dresses that he liked so I could try them on?" She hemmed and hawed and began pulling out dresses, saying, "This one's nice," and "This one's beautiful," and "This one was just made for you." She was the kind of salesperson that you would run from in a store because she would tell you that a grocery bag was designed just for you if it meant a sale.

Finally, when I became insistent that she show me what other dresses Vince had looked at, she looked at me fearfully and said, "Well, actually, he never came in. His secretary picked it out." Now I knew that the look that had crossed his face was one of pure dread in anticipation of one of my maddest moments. I stormed into his office with his credit receipt and let him know how thoughtless he really was. It didn't occur to me at the time to tell him also that, deep down, I was thankful he hadn't picked it out because I had always credited him with good taste and that dress certainly didn't meet the standards of good taste. I also didn't tell him that he had inadvertently taught me a valuable lesson: never let your temper keep you from exchanging a gift. I never replaced that dress, and it was certainly my loss. I learned that it's just not sensible to let hurt feelings get in the way of a new dress.

Christmas always seems to bring out the mischievous child in Vincent, and as I look back over the years, I guess he worked so long and so hard from August through December, he had to let his hair down at some point. What I will never understand is why I was always the butt of his jokes at Christmas, because he always had hell to pay before his pranks were finished. As I stated earlier, we always went to Birmingham for Christmas. For twenty years we packed up all the children, all the gifts, all the Santa Claus, and left home. Most of the time he was not in the best spirits, but we all wanted to go. It was five against one — majority rules — so we always loaded up and went.

My oldest brother, John, is married to one of the sweetest ladies who ever drew breath. She would never hurt anyone in any way and has always been referred to by the family as Saint Elaine. Vince has always teased Elaine and Kitty, my brother Mike's wife, about being the "outlaws" of the family and reminded them of how they had to stick together. Vince wrote the book on psychology, and here is how he drew Elaine into this particular Christmas plot. All I had asked for that year was a set of luggage, and I set out with a vengeance to help him remember. I told Vince in September that all I wanted for Christmas was luggage. I put signs in his suitcase. I wrote memos. I spared no effort to be sure he remembered that luggage. At some time during the holiday season, he called Elaine and commissioned her to purchase the luggage and have it at Mother's house so that I wouldn't find it. "Better still," Vince told Elaine, "put it in the trunk of your car and leave it there until I tell you I want it."

We got to Mother's house on the 23rd of December rather than the usual 24th, which gave us a day to play around and visit in Birmingham. That morning Vince asked Elaine and Kitty to go shopping with him, and I just knew they were going to buy the luggage I wanted. As they backed out of the driveway, I yelled, "Be sure its red!" (My mouth has gotten me in trouble more than once.) Well, ol' Vincent decided that he would really fix me. They went into a dime store in the area where he purchased a cameo ring — fake, of course. He had it gift-wrapped in a beautiful box. The three outlaws came home about three hours later and put my small gift under the tree. I saw that twinkle in Vince's eye, and I just knew that he didn't think about the luggage and had bought me what he wanted to buy. Glad? I couldn't wait to open presents that night.

After dinner, as was the custom, we all sat down as Santa began handing out the gifts. I noticed that the gift Vincent had put under the tree for me was being ignored, and it wasn't till all the gifts had been given out and opened that Santa happened to see that last little gift. "To Barbara," the little card said, "from Vincent . . . HO!HO!HO!" I excitedly took the gift, ripped it open, and looked down to see the cameo ring. My first reaction — since everybody was staring at me — was, "Oh isn't this beautiful . . . a cameo ring. I just love . . ." And then I saw that it had an adjustable band, like something out of a box of Cracker Jacks, and when I looked closer, I saw that the cameo was crooked. I looked up and saw that everyone was snickering at Vince Dooley's prank on me. Heartbroken and embarrassed, I just started crying. He had screwed up another Christmas for me.

Some say I had a hot temper in my youth, and I guess I still did because I unloaded in front of the whole family. I scared Elaine so badly that she turned a ghostly white, and I heard her whisper, "Please, Vince, tell her." I didn't know what there was to tell, but I knew I didn't want to hear anything from anybody; all I could do was cry. The next thing I knew, Vince took me outside, opened the trunk of Mother's car, and there was the luggage that I had wanted so desperately and had bugged him about for three months. I'm still not sure it was worth the effort or the suffering. I do know that to this day both Elaine and Kitty stay away from Vince's pranks, especially at Christmas.

I still remember the trucks that came down our driveway day after day during the six weeks Vince was away in the Far East. He went there on a coaching trip with Coach Erk Russell and left me at home alone with the four little ones. I think he felt so guilty about leaving that he tried to send parts of the Far East to our house from every place he visited. Whatever handiwork the town was famous for, he would by one of every color and mail it home. It was like Christmas every day, but his letters were what I looked forward to most. Each letter told all about the great baths he was getting—sometimes three a day—the great massages, all for about two American dollars. He was getting great baths and shopping in every great market in the Far East, and I was stripping down the cabinets in our kitchen and watching children to make the days go as fast as possible.

It was the middle of the week when a large truck delivered two huge crates. I couldn't imagine what treasure from the Orient this purchase could be. After going at it with a hammer and screwdriver, I finally resorted to calling Vince's nephew Bud to come help me, and we managed to open the crates. We stared at each other in disbelief as we extracted, not one, but two life-sized velvet nude paintings — one brunette and one redhead! "Oh my gosh," I thought, "the man has totally flipped out. The steam from all those baths has melted his brain." To this day I have no idea what possessed my analytical husband, whom I have credited with such good taste, to buy such a thing. Maybe he just got caught up in the thrill of shopping. But the most amazing thing was how proud he was of those paintings and what a great investment he thought he had made. All I could do was stash them in the attic before the children came home and saw them and hope they would somehow disappear.

But that wasn't the last of the Oriental velvets. A few years later, when the children got older and were playing in the attic, Daniel found them and brought them downstairs. "Hey, Mom," he asked, "what are these? I found them in the attic." I calmly said, "Those are your father's. You can ask him about them when he gets home." The minute Vince hit the door, the children started asking him about those naked women that Daniel found in the attic. I had on my "your sins have finally caught up with you" smirk when Vince said without flinching, "Golly, where are those pictures?"

"They're right here, Daddy," said the kids as they dragged him into the den.

"Yep, that's them, okay. Don't you guys recognize them?" "Daddy! Recognize naked women . . . us?"

"Well, yes," Vince said. "That's your mother. She paid her way through college posing for the art students." He had done it again — the old fourth-quarter finish.

Being the owner of two Oriental velvets should have prepared me, but I didn't know that I wasn't through with velvet paintings yet. Every spring for many years, a truck would stop at the corner of Alps Road and Broad Street in Athens with velvet paintings for sale. I passed that corner at least five times a day, and never once did I think about stopping, but that can't be said for the other members of my family. On Mother's Day one year the children sweetly brought my breakfast in bed, along with two of the biggest presents that they had ever given me. Both were wrapped in newspaper with ribbons, and I was tickled that they had gone to the effort of wrapping my gift and being so thoughtful. I opened the first — it was a velvet painting of a pink cat talking on the telephone. The other was the head of the crucified Christ! I tried to look like I loved them since the children were so proud of them. Vince rolled over in bed and whispered, "You're lucky. They wanted to get you a four-foot-long Last Supper!"

We were very fortunate that in our twenty-five years at Georgia we had only one losing season — in 1977. About two years before that, Vincent had given me an add-a-diamond bracelet with four diamonds in it, one representing each child. His intention was to add a diamond on special occasions until it was filled, but most of us know how that goes . . . you die with four diamonds in it. For some reason he forgets that promise, and even forgets he ever gave you the bracelet, or figures that's enough for a while and the while turns into decades. Anyway, I still had the four diamonds and realized that there would probably never be any more added to it.

Then came our losing season, and we ended up losing to Florida, Auburn, and Tech, all in a row. It was the absolute pits. It was the end of November, cold and rainy, and Vince had packed and left town to recruit for the next three weeks. I woke up on Monday morning in the depths of depression. I got the children off to school, and then began slowly getting dressed for the day. I spotted the diamond bracelet with the four diamonds on my dresser, picked it up and put it in my purse. I finished dressing and started to feel a little better. I must add that nothing helps my depression more than a good shopping trip—and I was in big depression. I headed for town and walked right into the jewelry store, pulled out the bracelet and said, "Fill 'er up, please." I didn't ask how much or how many. I just knew that I felt better; in fact, my depression completely left me.

I forgot all about that bracelet until Christmas Eve when the jeweler called to tell me it was ready. I almost died. I picked this beautiful thing up, along with a bill that I did not have the nerve to look at, and I came home plotting my strategy. There's an old joke among coaches' wives that if you want to buy something, always buy it during the season because your husband is so busy he won't notice until December or January and by then you can say you've had it for months. Why, I have friends who have actually bought living room and dining room furniture that went unnoticed during the season. Anyway, I figured that I had until January to break the news, and I wasn't sure when I was going to give him the bill. There would be a special time when I could spring it on him and it would be okay. I just had to bide my time.

But it was not to be. That afternoon Vince came into our bedroom and turned on the lights. We have a crystal fixture in the bedroom, and I had casually thrown the bracelet on the dresser. The prisms from the crystal caught the diamonds, and it was like dancing under the stars in our bedroom. Vince slowly walked over to the bracelet, held it up, and said, "Where in the hell did this come from?"

The children have always laughed at my voice when I get nervous — they call it "Mother's space voice" — and I was definitely in it now. I was talking a mile a minute about how depressed I was after the Tech game and how I figured that he had forgotten Christmas and on and on and on. I could tell that this was the maddest I had seen him in awhile, and I figured that I had better go on and give him the bill so I wouldn't have to go through this twice, so I ended with, "And here." He opened the sealed envelope and turned gray, then white. He put his index finger right between my eyes and said, "Young lady, I can never afford another losing season." The very next year we won the conference championship, and I take credit for that to this day.

It took Vince Dooley two years even to mention the diamond bracelet to me after the stunt I had pulled. One evening we were out having dinner together in a restaurant, just the two of us, and we were having a wonderful time. I picked up my water glass, and the bracelet was kind of dangling. He looked at it and said, "The least you could have done was have the thing cut down to fit your wrist. You could have saved me three diamonds."

Of course, I like to shop for Vince just as much as I like to shop for myself — or almost anyway. But it's not easy. In the first place, the Georgia people through the years have been wonderful to us and have sent us gifts year round. I bet we have everything red and black that has ever been made, and some of these things are probably one of a kind. Also, Vince is the kind of person who, if he wants or needs something, just goes out and buys it. He's not the kind of man who waits for a sale or waits for an occasion. But despite the difficulty, I take great delight in trying to surprise him for birthdays and Christmas with something special.

A few years ago I had decided that the one thing he needed that he didn't have was a big-screen, remote-control TV. Well, I spent weeks shopping for this machine. I compared the prices. I compared the speakers. I compared the screens. I compared everything you could compare, and I finally settled on one and had it delivered December 24. What a surprise! Not only was Vince ecstatic, but our boys were beside themselves. Now they could see football on a big-screen TV right in their home.

It was the most wonderful investment that I had ever made—our first remote-control gadget—and let me tell you, it has been a thorn in my side ever since. I don't know who invented the remote control, but I'm surely convinced that it was not a woman. I have never, ever had anything so distracting in my house. I don't think that in the past five years I have seen a complete TV show when Vince or any of my boys were at home, and I know for a fact that I have not seen a commercial in five years. I have no idea what they're selling on TV anymore. I don't even know how TV shows can get sponsors. If everybody in the world flips channels when commercials are on, why would anybody ever sponsor a show? I can't figure that out.

I have decided that men actually don't have an attention span over five minutes, and for some reason they can't stand to know that there is something going on on other channels that they are missing. So in order to cover the works, they go from station to station every three minutes, and that way they can watch every single thing on TV. I, on the other hand, go berserk after three flicks and finally just get up and walk out.

But I think the most ridiculous thing is when Vince says, "Well, let's go to bed." I get up to go, and he's flipping the TV around every channel one more time. That truly doesn't make sense to me, but he always wants to see what he's leaving for the night — just one last time.

One Sunday afternoon all of the children were off doing various things, and we were left alone in the house. He was sitting in his favorite chair watching his big-screen TV with his remote control in his hand. Most men I have observed assume the same position when they are watching TV. They have the remote control in one hand, and they have their other hand on their crotch. I have never in my life seen a woman sitting relaxed with her hand on her crotch, and I don't understand why men favor this position. But this is the natural position — be it husband, father, or male child. Anyway, there he was in that position, just in ecstasy, flipping his channels, hardly aware that I was in the room.

I decided that I would really fix him. So I got up, went to my bedroom, and put on my best makeup — the reddest, reddest rouge I could find, the brightest, gloppiest lipstick. I sprayed myself with my best perfume. I teased my hair up. Oh, I really looked hot. Then I wrapped myself in a beach towel, and I came out and stood between him and his big-screen TV. I dropped the towel and said, "Play me or trade me."

For one second he had a shocked look on his face; then he waved me aside and said, "Would you please move; you're making me miss a play."

"You wouldn't tell me to move if I were your second wife," I retorted.

"No," he said, "I'd never have the TV on if you were my second wife."

My Brand of Football

When you are in college sports, or any kind of sports for that matter, it becomes a way of life. Coaches and their families don't run on a normal calendar. A coach's calendar starts with recruiting, then spring practice, summer football camps, two-a-day practices, the football season, and, with luck, the year ends with a bowl game. This was a whole cycle, and we were consumed by every phase of it.

All my life I had been a sports fan of sorts because my father had been such an Alabama fan. He always had something bet on the game, and that spurred our interest. He was the kind of man who bet on everything. Nothing was fun unless he had a little money on it. Why, I'm not sure that he wouldn't bet on what time supper was if he could have gotten any takers. Shortly after Vince and I were married, we were home for the holidays, and all of us were sitting around talking about bowl games. Daddy very casually asked Vince if he wanted to bet on the game. Alabama was playing somebody in the Orange Bowl, and Vince said without hesitation, "Well, yes, I'll bet you two dollars on Alabama." Daddy took the bet and went to call his bookie. He had bet $100 on the other team, but now he was calling to bet $200 on Alabama. He later said that if Vince Dooley was willing to risk two dollars he knew it was a sure thing.

The first four years of our marriage I sat with the Auburn wives and learned all of my football manners from them. We were a rowdy bunch, hollering and yelling as though we could really affect the game by how much we got into it. I honestly knew nothing about football, and Vince says I still don't, but some of the wives were seasoned veterans. I would listen and try to pick up their lingo so that I would sound like a knowledgeable fan. "Watch that flanker." "Don't run a post." "Don't overshoot the hole." I didn't have the vaguest idea what they were talking about, but I had too much ego to let on. After one of the games we were all sitting around talking, and I had to blow my cover by chiming in, "Vincent, did you see that flanker almost run into the post?" He gave me a puzzled look, and everybody started laughing. It seems that my lot in life has always been to make people laugh, even at what I think are my most serious, intelligent moments. However, by the time I became the head coach's wife at the University of Georgia, I was schooled in watching football with the best of them.

The first game of Vince's career was against Coach Bear Bryant's Alabama team in Tuscaloosa with Joe Namath at quarterback. Vince was totally confident that we were going to win the game; he had me convinced. I had to stay home with the children, so I invited all the wives over to listen with me. We cooked dinner and then settled in to cheer for our first victory. Well, it didn't turn out quite that way. Alabama beat us, 33-3, and Vince believes to this day that Coach Bryant was merciful — it could have been a lot worse.

I crawled in bed feeling sick over the defeat, said my prayers, and then wondered what I could say to console my husband when he got in from the game. "What does a head coach's wife say when her husband has just gotten a whippin'?" I thought and thought and drifted off to sleep with a variety of comforting phrases rolling around in my brain. It had been a night game, and about three-thirty in the morning I heard Vince slowly climbing the steps to the bedroom. When he sat down on the bed to take off his shoes, I rolled over, but all I could think to say was "How did it go?" He started laughing and then I started laughing, and that broke the ice and eased both of us through a tense moment.

It's funny how through the years certain games stand out in your mind. For me, it was not whether we won or lost, but events that took place surrounding the game that would make it memorable for me. Of course, a football coach doesn't remember events; he remembers the score. I've never understood how a man could recall every score of every football game that he ever coached but can't remember the birth dates of his children or his own anniversary or even Christmas!

In the seventies we were playing Alabama in Tuscaloosa and I was determined to get there. By now I was a seasoned coach's wife in that I had learned to do everything by myself during the football season and never to depend on my husband for anything. Any time your husband could give you was a bonus. You certainly couldn't expect anything, and if you did, you were sure to be disappointed.

Before I start this little story, I must explain that Vince Dooley never believed in letting the wives travel with the coaches or the team to a game. If I wanted to go to an out of town game I had to get there on my own. He never believed in mixing business with pleasure. In fact, even if we could get to the out of town games, for many years he wouldn't let the wives stay in the rooms with their husbands. I thought it was absolutely ridiculous, but he was winning, and you don't fix something that isn't broken. He was a hero, and who was I to challenge his philosophy — at least at this time in my life?

The Florida game was the only one of the year that he allowed the wives to attend at the expense of the Athletic Department, but we had to fly commercial and we had to stay together. He did not want his coaches caught up in marital problems the night before a game. Some of the most fun we had was on those Florida game trips. I remember vividly the year we beat Florida in the pouring rain with Mike Cavan as our quarterback. I had on a white knit dress — back then you dressed up to go to football games — and a bright red vinyl raincoat. The wetter I got, the longer my dress got; when I stood up to leave the game what had started as a normal hemline was around my ankles. When we got to the airport, giddy with victory and soaking wet, I took off my coat and found that my white knit dress was pink. The coat had faded all over me. Ah, what price victory!

Now, getting back to that Alabama game that I was determined to go to: I couldn't leave on Friday like everyone else because Daniel was playing football at Clarke Central on Friday night and Deanna was cheering. I made a major point of supporting everything the children did because I felt that I had to be both father and mother, especially during football season. I fretted and fretted about how I was going to get to the game. Finally, the

Monday morning before the game I said to Vincent, as he was glancing over the morning paper before running out the door, "I've tried and tried to get to the game Saturday, and I just can't figure out a way to get there. Do you have any suggestions?"

He looked a little irritated at me and said, "I can't be worrying about how you're going to get to the football game. I have a hundred players to worry about and a staff of coaches. If you want to go bad enough, you'll find a way." That did nothing but push my back to the wall, and he was right: I would find a way. I immediately picked up the telephone and called Augusta Aviation. They had charter service, and I rented myself an airplane. I figured that Vince wouldn't get the bill for a month, and it would be too late to do anything about it. They were scheduled to pick me up at eight o'clock Saturday morning . . . perfect! Saturday morning came, and as I was dressing, the phone rang. It was the pilot. "Mrs. Dooley, Athens is all socked in, and it doesn't look like its going to lift until about noon." I almost died. I had to get to that game. Friday night I had heard that Deanna's cheerleading coach and her husband were driving over Saturday morning, being the big Bulldog Boosters that they were, so at 7:45 a.m. I called and asked for a ride. They said they would be glad to have me but they weren't coming back until Monday." I told them that was okay; if they would just get me there, I would find a way home.

Off we went. I was finally on my way to Tuscaloosa, Alabama, and I had done it by myself. As we were heading down I-20, right before we got to the Pell City exit, the drive shaft fell out of the car. After walking to the exit and all the way up the ramp looking for help, we finally flagged down an Alabama sheriff. Now, I'm from Alabama and I've seen how some Southern sheriffs are depicted. This one was a cloned Alabama sheriff! He weighed about three hundred pounds, had a full beard and mustache, and was wearing his flat-top hat. His badge was on his bosom and his gun was on his hip. We told him our plight, and he looked us over while rubbing his mangy beard. Finally, he said "Well, folks, hit's Saradey and everthing closes 'bout noon 'round here."

I knew by his attitude we were in for a long haul, but I had come too far to miss the kickoff now. I began walking down the exit ramp with Jean and Roger following me. I told them that I appreciated the ride but I was not hanging around Pell City. I was getting to the game. I began thumbing, and immediately a car with two men in it stopped.

"Lady, you need a ride?"

"Sure do," I said. "You going near Tuscaloosa?"

"That's exactly where we're heading. Hop in."

Well, Jean and Roger, being very protective of me and also being major-league Bulldog fans, jumped in with me, and we took off down the road. The two men introduced themselves, and I introduced Jean and Roger and then said, "I'm Barbara Dooley." The driver turned his head all the way to the back and asked, "THE Barbara Dooley?"

"Yes," I said, "Barbara Dooley."

He looked at me through the rear view mirror and said, "Vince Dooley's Barbara Dooley?"

"Yes."

"Lady," he said, "you sure have a cheap husband."

Later that week I wrote him a note thanking him for picking me up and taking me to the game, and shortly thereafter he wrote back telling me how much he appreciated the letter because his wife didn't believe a word of that story.

Alabama games always thrilled me. I guess it stemmed from my roots and how we were always so excited when Auburn played Alabama. Now, I will have to say that I only went to two Auburn games in Auburn during the entire twenty-five years that Vince coached. We lost both of them. I went in 1964, Vince's first year at Georgia, and I was thrilled to be going back and seeing all of the friends I had left behind a few months before. They had been to the Orange Bowl, and I wanted to hear all about that, and I had had Denise and wanted to show pictures of our second daughter.

I was hyped to see them and super-hyped about Vincent going against our alma mater and against our friend Coach Jordan. Plus, I was confident we would win, and I wanted to be able to gloat after our victory. Oh, does God have a way of humbling the proud.

The only other time I returned to the Loveliest Village was in 1988. I wanted to go because it was Vince's last year and I was confident he was going to go out as the conference champion; I wanted to be with him to savor the final victory against our great rival. It wasn't to be, and I must say that that loss to Auburn was the hardest that I personally have ever felt. I wanted the championship so much for Vincent. I had prayed so hard, and I just knew God would grant the story-book ending I wanted. We never know God's ways, but I do know that most of the time it's not the way I would write the script. I never want to go back to that stadium again.

The other Alabama game that stands out so vividly in my mind was the year we played Alabama at Legion Field in Birmingham. Home for the weekend against Alabama and I couldn't wait. What excitement! Birmingham is such a fun football-weekend town; everyone really gets into the spirit of the game, just like a college town should. I went home and stayed with Mama while Vince stayed with the team in a hotel.

It was certainly not an unusual football weekend as most of them go. It was on national TV, which made it a little more exciting, but there was no indication to me that this would be a turning point in Vince Dooley's life.

Those who have followed Georgia football know how conservative Coach Dooley has always been in his play calling. The pattern is pretty familiar: first down, hand-off; second down, hand-off; third down, hand-off; fourth down, punt. If you can't control the ball, then wait for the other team to make the mistake. "Great philosophy," I had always sneered. This day was to be different. It seems like his whole personality changed when he played an Alabama team. Maybe this stemmed from his earlier years, too, of always having Alabama as his chief rival when he was the quarterback and then a coach at Auburn.

As the first quarter progressed, I felt that this was going to be a strange day. But little did I know that Vince would be going through his midlife crisis in living color on national TV. Most men, when they get to this stage in their lives, will give you some signs of male menopause. The first clue is removing the tie and unbuttoning the first two buttons of the shirt. That lasts awhile, and then you see him brush a couple of strands of chest hair to make them peek out of his shirt and look really sexy. A few months later he will add a gold chain or two to adorn his neck. Next he'll trade the family sedan in for a sports model, and you know he's hopeless when he puts on the little plaid sports cap!

Vince had none of these signs, but here he was on national TV, in my hometown, with a full-blown case of middle-age crazies. Three times on fourth down and one, he went for it! Unbelievable. Now it was late in the game, about three minutes left on the clock, and we had the ball on our own 30-yard line. All of a sudden it was another fourth down and one situation, and everyone in the stands started yelling in disbelief, "He's going for it . . . he's going for it." We were ahead by three points with the ball back in our own territory, and I knew he was crazy if he went for it. Why, all they had to do was kick a field goal and they would tie us. There was no way . . . I knew him too well.

I looked down on the field . . . no kicker in sight. They were going for it. "Oh," I thought, "he couldn't be that stupid!" As I sat in the fetal position with my eyes shut, they lined up and went for it. They didn't make it. Now we were really in a bind. All Alabama had to do was line up, kick a field goal, and the game would be tied. But thankfully, that was not Coach Bryant's style. Alabama came out of the huddle to win the game, and they started throwing: first down . . . incomplete; second down . . . incomplete; third down and we intercepted in the end zone, and only through that interception were we able to win the game.

Well, everyone was celebrating and cheering, and I was still in shock. I couldn't believe that my smart husband had made such a poor choice of calls, and I couldn't wait to tell him about it. The minute the game was over I took off for the dressing room to challenge his competence. As I approached the dressing room area, jammed with screaming, rejoicing fans, there Vincent stood with a circle of reporters and cameramen around him hanging on his every word. If you win—no matter how you win—you're a hero and a genius. He saw me coming and, after our long years together, could tell from a glance that I was hot . . .

and coming after him with the hard questions. He looked
up from the adoring press and cameras and, without paus-
ing, stared me straight in the face, pointing his finger in
my direction, and said, "See if I'm ever going to listen to
you again."

The Georgia Tech game has always been special to the
Georgia people because beating Tech conferred year-long
bragging rights throughout the state. I can remember so
vividly our first year at Georgia in 1964 when we beat Tech
between the hedges here in Athens. My dad and two of his
buddies from Birmingham came over and escorted me to
the game. Dad was in heaven over having his son-in-law
the head coach at the University of Georgia. In fact, the
year before, when Vince told the family that had been
named the coach, my dad's reply was, "Son, I'd rather you
be the head football coach at Georgia than President of
the United States." (Through the years I have often
thought about that statement and just wondered if the
President really has as much pressure.) After the game was
over, the Georgia fans were wild. We had beaten Tech, and
this young coach was alright. Meanwhile, the Tech fans
were in disbelief. How could this happen to them and
Coach Dodd? We were all rowdy leaving the stadium,
totally full of victory and just wanting to walk around and
savor it with everyone there. Dad had a sign that said,
"Vince Dooley for President." A Tech man, dressed from
top to bottom in white and gold with yellow jackets all over
him, came up and said, "Hell yes, I'll vote for him. I'll even
contribute . . . anything to get him out of Athens."

That first year was so special. In fact, I doubt if there will
ever again be anything in my life so perfectly ideal. Our
invitation to the Sun Bowl made it a real fairy-tale year.
The Sun Bowl . . . we were all ecstatic. I don't think that I

had ever been any further west than Mississippi, and here we were going to El Paso. The staff and team were being rewarded for a job well done, and no one could have been more appreciative than we were. The Sun Bowl that year was played the day after Christmas, which meant that we all had to leave before Christmas and wouldn't be home until December 27. There was not one complaint; no one had a single misgiving about not being home for Christmas. Our children were so young that one day was just like the next unless we told them otherwise, so we had Christmas the day before we left for Texas. Mother cooked the big dinner, we opened all of our presents to each other, we sang songs and got ready for Santa. On December 22 Santa came to the Dooleys' and all the other coaches' houses, and no one ever missed a beat. We had done it all. The only problem was that our neighbors' children couldn't understand why Santa had come to the Dooleys' and not been to their house that night. Children and spouses of coaches do learn to adapt to most anything.

We left for El Paso full of excitement and anticipation. The state of Georgia had sent us off with glorious write-ups and many congratulations. The Georgia people were intoxicated with this new attitude of winning, and we were soaking it all up in every pore of our bodies. That first staff had to be the best that has ever been together anywhere. We all came into the situation not really knowing how we would do, knowing only that we had a four-year contract and that the Georgia people would not tolerate another losing program. We had a closeness and a camaraderie that we never had again. The players even felt this unity and knew that we were all winners together. Christmas Eve night in El Paso we heard caroling outside our window. I opened the curtains and saw Pat Hodgson, Lyn Hughes, and Kirby Moore serenading us. We were all family.

I have to admit that I did cry on Christmas morning when I woke and didn't have our children with us. I felt a little guilty until I called and found out that Santa Claus had been to see them again at Nana and Pop's house and that this Santa must be a lot richer 'cause they got everything they wanted. We beat Texas Tech in El Paso and headed home to spend the first day of 1965 with our children and our new friends in Athens.

The new year started out fine, but as the football season approached, it turned sour. One week before we opened with Alabama in Athens, my father died. We buried him one week exactly before the opening game, and I immediately felt cheated that he would not be with me this second season, or any other season, to share the victories and the defeats with me. I don't think anyone is ever ready to give up a parent, but the loss of a young, vital parent is truly a shock, and this was a shock!

Seven days later we beat Alabama on what was then — and to some still is — a controversial play called the "flea-flicker." With only minutes left, our receiver caught a pass and immediately flipped the ball to a man trailing behind him. The play went for a touchdown . . . we had pulled the game out. Everyone in the stadium went berserk. We had done it . . . we had beaten the Bear . . . we had beaten Alabama. All I could do was stand there in silence as tears streamed down my face. I knew, without a doubt, that my dad had been at the game. I knew that somehow he had pulled this win off just to let me know that all was okay and that he would be at every game. In later years I often wondered whether he gave up football for some other heavenly hobbies — because there were times when we needed him and he didn't come through.

Remembering my dad's passing reminds me of a funny story about my mother. I mentioned earlier that my dad was a betting, fun-loving man. Mother would always fuss at him about his gambling habits and about his fun, and he would always say to Vince, "Women — they just can't stand to see their husbands have a good time." Vince has always remembered that famous quote and has reminded me of it more than once.

As much as Mama fussed at Daddy about his gambling, he never stopped. It wasn't two weeks after we buried Daddy that Mother called and started talking football. My mother talking football . . . I couldn't believe it. I told Vince about it, and at first he found it rather amusing. But each Thursday Mom would call and ask about the team, and I would tell her everything I could think of. Finally, Vince said to me, "Your mother is betting on the games. You cannot talk to her again about my team."

"You've got to be crazy," I said. "Mother doesn't even know what a point-spread is." He told me to ask her point-blank. I did.

"Well, sure I'm betting on the games," she responded. "They're no fun unless you have a little something on them."

I almost passed out. Here she was calling me every week to see who was hurt, who was going to start, and what we thought about the opponent. Needless to say, those phone calls stopped, but her betting didn't.

Georgia Tech has always been our last game of the season and has always set the tone for the off-season and the holidays. If you beat Tech you knew Christmas would be good, recruiting would be better, and the next twelve months in the state would be great. In 1975 we played Tech in Atlanta on Thanksgiving night. This meant that Vince would take the team over on Wednesday before the game and we would have to spend Thanksgiving without him and then drive to Atlanta.

We left Athens about two o'clock Thursday afternoon with the intention of stopping at a nice restaurant in Atlanta and having Thanksgiving dinner; that way it would be special even if Vince weren't with us. Back in those days eating in any restaurant was special to us. When you are raising four children you have many rules; if you didn't, life would not be bearable. Those of you with large families know that you enforce the rules with the oldest children, but by the time the baby comes along you really become lax. We were no exception. Vincent had a rule that our oldest boy could not come down on the sidelines during a game until he was ten years old. But Derek, the baby, wanted to get down there when he was four. This Thanksgiving Day he was six, and all the way to Atlanta he was bugging me about getting on the sidelines. I finally said, "Derek, your daddy is probably feeling guilty about not being with us on Thanksgiving, so I bet that if you ask him when we get to the hotel, he might let you." Mothers have a great way of setting up their husbands.

Just as I thought, Vince was in a soft mood, and when Derek asked him about going to the sidelines, he smiled and said, "I'll tell you what, Derek; if we are beating Tech by a large enough score at the end of the third quarter, your mother can walk you down to the fence and get a manager to get you over and you can stay on the sidelines during the fourth quarter. But there will be two rules: you can't get near me, and you can't get near the team." Compromise has always been one of Vince's strong points, and here he had masterfully done it again. Derek was pleased and gave older brother Daniel a look that said, "Ha ha ha; I'm gonna get down there tonight whether I'm ten years old or not."

Ever since our children were old enough to pray, we have had family prayers each night. Vince was rarely at home, but we would sit down and pray for the world, for the family, for our friends, for our dog, whatever they wanted to pray about. It was a special time for our family, and a normal fifteen-minute prayer period could end up being an hour-long rap session. It was good and healthy for us; the phone would be off the hook, the TV was off, dinner was over, homework was done, and it was our time. I must confess that we always prayed before ballgames, no matter who was in the house. We took a few minutes to gather and talk to the Lord about the outcome of the game. We didn't care who the best team was. We prayed to win. This particular night was no different. In Atlanta, in a hotel room that Thanksgiving night, 1975, we all knelt down for our prayer time. Then Derek, as only a child could do, said, "and Jesus, please let us be beating Tech by a big enough score in the third quarter that I can get to the sidelines."

At the end of the third quarter we were leading Tech by a score of 42-0, and I thought that was a big enough lead to take Derek to the sidelines. Before we started down — and I must say that he had been ready since the half — I went over the rules one more time: "You can't get near your dad and you can't get near his players. Do you understand." "Yes, ma'am," was his eager reply, so off we went to the sidelines.

By the time that we got to the fence at Grant Field, Tech had scored to make it 42-7. By the time I got a manager to lift Derek over the fence, it was 42-14. I climbed through the crowds and got back to my seat just as the crowd let out a roar. Tech had scored again, and it was now 42-21. Tech kicked an on-sides kick and recovered the ball, and I looked down to see Derek pulling on his father's pants leg. I almost died. Tech was going right down the field, five yards at a time, and I was watching Vince kick Derek and try to push him away. But Derek hung tough and stayed right with him. I knew there was nothing I could do now, but I also knew that I was going to be in serious trouble for not disciplining "my" child to understand what he could and couldn't do. Finally, after what seemed an eternity, Tech scored to make the score 42-28, and I saw Vince lean down and exchange words with Derek. Then I watched Derek prance to the bench where he sat the remainder of the game.

We won the game that night, and I vowed never to mention the sidelines to Vince again. We went back to the Riviera Hotel, our refuge for many years in Atlanta when we played Tech, where we had a two-bedroom suite. We put the children to bed in one room and we crawled into our bed exhausted from the evening but exhilarated. Vince reached over and turned out the lights. It was pitch-black in the room, with a stillness of death hanging in the air. I knew that something major was about to be said, and I wasn't sure I wanted to hear it. I drew my elbows as tight as I could against my ribs, hoping that he couldn't hear me breathe and would forget that I was in the bed. But no such luck.

"Barbara," he said at last in a clear, demanding voice.

I froze, and my Adam's apple felt like it was the size of a grapefruit. I could hardly get my voice out, and I really wanted to say, "Sir," but I didn't. In the clearest voice I could muster, I managed to say, "What?"

"The darnedest thing happened on the sidelines tonight," Vince said. "There I was in the heat of battle. Tech had the ball on their last scoring drive, and Derek was pulling on my pants leg. I kicked him . . . I tried shoving him. I did everything I could to shake him, and I finally leaned down and said, 'Derek, what do you want?' Barbara, he looked up at me with those big brown eyes and said, 'Dad, don't worry about a thing. Jesus is just out here having a little fun.'"

The following summer, as the August two-a-days got underway, an interesting story started to develop. Sometimes the kids get together in August and decide to do something special for team unity or team spirit, and this year a few of them got together and decided to shave their heads. There are not many wonderful-looking bald heads after the age of three months, and this group was certainly no exception. Coach Erk Russell had always had a bald head and looked terrific; in fact, I'm not sure that hair would look good on him. But here, going into the season, we had a whole group of bald heads. I thought it was funny and a grand idea for the players, and it seemed to work. We were winning games, and after each victory a new player or coach would get shaved. Of course, the scalp everybody wanted was Coach Dooley's, and at the beginning of the season he had promised that if we won the conference championship, and went on to beat Tech, he would shave his head.

Now I can remember stories about Grant Teaff of Baylor motivating his team by eating a live worm, but shaving your head? That's pretty extreme, especially when you spend most of your time and money trying not to lose your hair. The inevitable did happen . . . we won the SEC and went on to beat Tech! Now Vince had to live up to his commitment. But when? The team was ready to take him up on his word right after the Tech game, but somehow he escaped.

Now he came home and decided that we had to have a plan. The Touchdown Club of Athens was hosting a championship celebration in December, and he decided he would shave it that day and surprise everyone. He wouldn't let me do it; he always has to have a professional, no matter what we need done. So I called the girl who cut my hair, let her in on the secret, and asked if she would come to our house at 5:00 on the appointed day. She would have an hour to do the job, and we would be ready to go to the party at 7:00. It was all set. Next he decided that he needed a wig because he couldn't spend the winter with a bald head, so I looked in the Atlanta yellow pages and saw an ad for men's hair pieces. The artistic stylist was John Salvadori, who has since, along with his wife, Mary, become our friends. I called and identified myself, asked about wigs, and told him confidentially what Vince's plan was. He said that Vince needed to come in before he shaved his head so they would match up color; then he could cut the hair piece the same way Vince wore his natural hair and no one would ever know. The wig was ordered and styled and waiting on this memorable December night.

Shaving Vince's head was a hoot. We all got in the bathroom laughing like silly kids, and at first we all took a turn with the razor. Then Vince got nervous at all the fun we were having and ran the children out of the room, leaving me there to take pictures with the beautician. One hour later the deed was done, and we dressed and went to the party with Vince in his new wig.

It was strange how everyone knew that something was different about Vince but no one could actually put their finger on the difference. "Vince you look tired," somebody would say, or, "Hey, Vince, you've gained weight this season," or, "Vince, you've sure lost a lot of weight this season." People would look, but they just weren't quite sure about what was different.

Then it happened. He got up and started recapping the year, built the story up to a crescendo, and at the very end yelled, "Hail to the Champs" as he yanked his wig off. I know that if I live another hundred years I will never be in a room filled with such wild emotion. Everybody leaped to their feet, knocking over tables and chairs, cheering, throwing their napkins in the air, laughing and shoving to get to the head table just to be near him. The photographers were having a field day. What started out to be a nice celebration turned into one of the best parties anyone would ever remember. Their head coach had lived up to his promise and had done it his way!

I can remember so vividly rolling over the next morning and seeing that baby-bald skinhead on the pillow and almost dying of shock. In the reality of morning it looked awful. The thought that I had to look at that naked dome until it grew out made me want to throw up. And what if it didn't grow out? It did, however, and actually came in thicker than before, but Vince spent the whole winter complaining of a cold head, and I spent the whole winter threatening him about ever making such a promise again. But in the meantime, he was the hero, and he had lived up to his word. His players and coaches loved him. From that day on he has always been able to empathize with bald-headed men, but I know for a fact that he set bald heads back at least fifty years.

I should add here that wearing a wig made Vince feel years younger. It was amazing how putting a lot of hair on his bald head made him return to his youth, to the time when he actually did have a lot of hair. I never really knew him then, but he swears he did have a thick head of hair, and every time he looks at Daniel's thick, curly hair, he reminds him that one day his will go, too.

Shortly after he shaved his head, we went to Atlanta to a banquet. He wore his new wig and was really feeling like hot stuff. A thick head of hair and a conference championship—what could be better in life? On our way home, he put his arm around me as he drove. He hadn't done that since we got married, and I looked at him in shock. He got a strange look on his face and asked, "How long has it been since we've parked?" He pulled off the interstate and began to kiss me, and I realized that this new-found head of hair was just too much stimulation. So, as he was kissing me, I pulled his wig off, and within one minute he was fast asleep. I kind of liked my baldheaded Vincent.

THE YEAR THAT WAS

Since 1979 was one of the few years—in fact, very few years—that we had not gone to a bowl, 1980 got off to an unusual start. We spent a very quiet Christmas and then rented a van and took the family, plus Derek's best friend, Hamp McWhorter, to North Carolina skiing. It was a typical Dooley trip. Wherever we go, when Vince plans a trip, he calls someone in the area so that he or she can make our arrangements. On this particular trip he called Coach Bill Bomar, who has since died, but who was one of the all-time greatest people we had ever met.

Coach Bomar had it all planned for us. The first couple of days the boys—Vince, Daniel, Derek, and Hamp—would stay at Lees-McRae College, which was closed for the holidays, and the girls—Deanna, Denise, and I—would stay at his home in the mountains. We would ski at Sugar Mountain, where he had passes for the day lined up for us. It was going to be fun! We always start our family trips with a positive attitude, but by midway, mutiny arises among the troops, usually led by the women.

Derek has been skiing since he was four years old, thanks to my brother John and his family. They have a son, Gavin, who's one year older than Derek, and they are as close as brothers, so every time Johnny would take his family skiing, Derek was invited to go. On the other hand, Daniel had never had the opportunity, and this was to be his first experience on the slopes. Deanna had been one time and knew only the basics, so this was going to be Derek's opportunity to show his stuff.

The minute we got there we put them all in a group lesson, and Vince and I proceeded to leave them and ski. Derek came with us and would periodically check on the others and report back to us with hysterical tales and laughter. Finally, on our last run before lunch, as we were riding up the lift, Vince looked to his left and saw Daniel standing against the fence with his cowboy boots and cowboy hat on and what was obviously a plug of tobacco in his mouth. Here was our sixteen-year-old displaying defiance, though of course he wasn't smart enough to realize that we would see him before he spit the tobacco out. He was being Mr. Cool for his audience, whoever that might be.

Vince nudged me and said, "Look at your son. What the hell does he think he's doing?"

I started laughing and said, "Looks to me like your son has quit." That was all I needed to say to aggravate an already touchy situation.

When we skied down, we flew right past Daniel at the fence and told him to gather the troops and to meet us for lunch. Vince was showing no signs of anger. This is another one of his great qualities—or maybe sometimes his weakness; he is able to suppress his feelings until the appropriate time or until he has sorted them out in his mind. That way, when he does tell you how he feels, he can also tell you without regret or second-guessing what he expects done about the situation.

We took our skis off and walked to the fence where Daniel was standing, the plug of tobacco no longer in evidence. Vince looked at him and said, "Son, what do you think you are doing?" Daniel said that the instructor had tried to teach him to snowplow and it killed his knees. Daniel had had two knee operations by this time in his life, and there was even some talk about implanting artificial kneecaps at some later time if his knees continued to give him trouble. So he had a legitimate complaint about his knees, but his arrogant attitude was what Vince couldn't tolerate. After trying to snowplow down the baby hill for an hour, Daniel had quit . . . totally given up . . . and that's not an attitude for the Dooley family!

We had lunch laughing and talking about how the children's morning had been and listening to what they had learned, how many times they had fallen, and all the stories that make family trips fun — everyone jawing about everyone else. Daniel all the while maintained that he had finished . . . until we got ready to go out again and Vince said, "Daniel, get on your gear. You're coming up with me." Daniel said that he wasn't interested, that he had quit; his knees hurt and he didn't want to ski. Vincent then proceeded to tell him how much money we had spent to get there — renting the equipment, the lessons — and informed him that there was no way he was quitting, knees or no knees. Daniel knew then that he was going up the slopes because when Vince makes that kind of a statement, you don't argue.

On went the equipment, and Vince literally pushed Daniel to the lift. Here is my son who has never been on a lift, and his Dad is telling him that there's nothing to it; he'll get him off and get him down the hill. Of course, Daniel fell getting off the lift, but Vince helped him up and got him to the spot where you start down the mountain. That was the last bit of help Daniel received. Vince gave him a quick verbal lesson, and then they started down. Daniel fell immediately, and Vince came up behind him, ordered him to get up, and jabbed him with his pole. Daniel fell again, and Vince came up behind him and jabbed him again. Finally, after about four quick falls, Daniel began skiing, and when he did fall leaped up before the pole could get to him. To this day Daniel can get up from a fall faster than most people can fall down. Daniel loves to ski now, by the way, and had his father not been so persistent, he might never have learned.

It was a good trip — great family time — but it was also disappointing not to be at a bowl. We came home on December 31 so that we could inhale all of the bowl action on New Year's Day. As was our tradition, we stopped at a grocery store on our way home and bought a can of black-eyed peas to eat that night, the old wives' tale being that you never bring in the New Year without black-eyed peas or you'll have bad luck. We sure didn't want any more bad luck; we wanted to be at a bowl next New Year's Day.

For about five years I had been bugging Vince about taking me to Marriage Encounter, a movement in our church that "makes good marriages better." It's a weekend during which couples focus totally on one another for two full days and two nights, and I knew that we needed it. He kept saying that there was nothing wrong with our marriage and that he didn't need that. I insisted we did. Finally, in August of 1979, when he asked me what I wanted for my birthday, in September — or maybe he didn't ask — I told him that he wouldn't have to worry about my birthday if he would just put Marriage Encounter on his calendar for March of 1980 and block that weekend out . . . for me. That was all I wanted.

When you put something on your calendar that far ahead, you don't think that it will ever come. Plus, you don't think that you will actually have to do it when the time comes. He thought that I would back out by then, so he said that would be fine. And he blocked the designated weekend off of his calendar.

The first part of the year was especially intense for us because that was the climax of our efforts to recruit Herschel Walker. Herschel didn't sign on signing date like most players do; he was going to wait. What Herschel didn't know was how greatly he affected so many families during this period of uncertainty. That was literally the only thing on Vince's mind — how we were going to sign Herschel? It was the big topic of conversation among our alumni, our fans, the sportswriters — Herschel Walker. I can't ever remember being so affected by the recruiting of any one person in the whole twenty-five years that we were at Georgia. I honestly got sick of hearing about it, and I sure didn't want to read any more words about it. Grown men were acting like fools trying to get an eighteen-year-old boy to tell them he loved them the best.

One night Vince crawled into bed — late — after having been on the phone with Coach Mike Cavan, the coach who had been delegated to "live" with Herschel, to do whatever it took, within the rules, to get him signed. I was aggravated that when Vince did get home he would spend hours on the phone talking about Herschel, so I bolted up and said, "If I were you, I would tell Herschel to shove it. We don't need him anyway."

Vince responded like a scorned lover: "Don't you ever say that again, and you'd better not ever let anyone know you think that."

As usual, he was right. We did need Herschel, and whatever it took was worth it. Hindsight is amazingly keen.

One afternoon about four o'clock Vince was home packing to go to Wrightsville to see Herschel when the phone rang. It was an Atlanta sportswriter.

"Barbara," he pleaded, "I need a fresh story on Herschel. Surely you can give me something new."

Vince was hurriedly packing, ignoring me, and I thought I would get a rise out of him. I was on the bedroom phone, so there was no way he couldn't hear every word I was saying. "Herschel Walker?" I replied in a nice loud voice. "Why, Coach Dooley and I never talk about Herschel Walker. We're too busy either talking about making love or making love."

Vince looked at me in total shock and began frantically waving his hands to get me to shut up. When the reporter stopped laughing and I got off the phone, Vince said, "Why would you say something like that? Don't you know that he'll print that garbage?"

"If you're lucky he will," I retorted, "and it'll change your image."

March came, and what a relief! Herschel still had not signed, but our weekend had finally come, and I was excited about going to Marriage Encounter. Vince was reluctant and had made a number of attempts to get out of it, but I held firm. The letter came with the information for the weekend, and the first instruction was Do Not Be

Late! We were told to be sure to leave enough time to avoid holding the group up. The mandated arrival time was seven o'clock on Friday night.

I had reminded Vince several times about the particulars and had told him that we absolutely must not be late. He was to pick me up at five, which would give us two hours to get to Atlanta. It usually took about an hour and a half, so we had some insurance that we would be there on time. Five o'clock came and went, and Vince was not here to pick me up. At quarter to six he finally drove up, making excuses about being on the phone about Herschel and pointing out that he really shouldn't be leaving town at such a crucial time. I was calm. I had prayed about it so hard and so long that I knew we would be going . . . the Lord had not brought me this far to let me down now. I just had to keep my cool. I kept a smile on my face as we loaded the car and headed to Atlanta.

Right outside of Atlanta he looked at his watch and said, "I'll tell you what . . . we're so late now, let's just the two of us go have a quiet dinner together somewhere and head on back home." He had turned his charm on and was trying to buy me off, but I held firm.

"No," I replied. "I don't care how late we are. We are going."

I don't even remember where the motel was, but we got to the right Howard Johnson's, and there was a man in the parking lot with a Marriage Encounter tag on his coat and a huge smile on his face directing us into our space. Vince cut his eyes at me and said, "Who is that silly ass?" I knew he wanted to run, but he had made a commitment to me, and there was no way he was going to back out now.

It proved to be a wonderful experience for us both but really an eye-opener for me. For years I had thought that I was the perfect wife and mother and that I was the only one in the marriage with anything to complain about. It's a real revelation to hear, in a loving atmosphere, your partner's thoughts as to your faults and shortcomings. I wasn't the only one who thought things needed working on. Our marriage wasn't perfect and probably never would be. Our marriage was good, and we wanted it to be better. This was certainly a start.

You would think that on a weekend such as this I would find no way to put my foot in my mouth, but I managed. Usually during these Marriage Encounter weekends, they will have one or two priests going through the experience just as the couples do. It teaches them better communication skills and also gives them a much deeper insight into married life. At each meal you are seated with different people so that you can get to know the group, and as fate would have it, the second day at lunch we were at the table with a priest from Mississippi. He asked us about our parish, and we found that we knew some of the same people in Mobile. In fact, he knew one of Vince's friends who was now the Archbishop of the Mobile-Birmingham diocese. Anyway, one thing led to another, and I proceeded to tell him my thoughts on our then-Bishop Donnellan.

"You wouldn't believe this man," I ranted. "I believe that he hates women. I got so angry at some of his policies that I just barged into his office one day and told him what I thought of how he treated our parish in Athens."

I went on and on, and he just listened quietly. Meanwhile Vince was saying, "Now, Barbara, don't exaggerate. He isn't that bad. Give the man a break." He turned to the priest and said, "Father, when Barbara gets down on someone, it takes her a long time to get off his back."

The more Vince tried to smooth the troubled waters, the more I would say. Finally lunch was over, and I never thought another thing about our conversation with the priest from Mississippi. The next day at our closing Mass, as we stood for the priest to enter, I looked up and there coming down the aisle was the priest we had had lunch with the day before, but something was noticeably different. He had a bishop's miter on his head.

Vince gently grabbed my arm and whispered, "You've done it again."

I couldn't pray for trying to recall all the things that I had said about our bishop. It was obvious that this man was his friend, and they had probably worked closely together at Southern Bishops' Conferences. I finally managed to pray, "Lord, you gave me this mouth. Why can't it be nice?"

Of course, after Mass I approached him to apologize but also to chide him for not telling us who he was: "That was a dirty trick keeping your identity a secret." He just laughed and gently kissed my cheek and told me to "go in peace and sin no more."

Arriving back home on Sunday night, we felt like we were on a honeymoon until we walked in the door and the phone started ringing about Herschel. Vince immediately had a meeting, and new discussions and plans were underway. We had to have Herschel. During this time my brother Michael and his family were living in Boston. He was doing his residency there and had been inviting us up, but we could never really find a time. I decided that I couldn't take much more of this Herschel thing and that during the Easter Holidays I would take the children to Washington, Boston, and New York. We planned to be gone a week, but I told Vince that we wouldn't be home until he signed Herschel.

That trip was something all of us will always remember. We all had specific jobs. Daniel would be the main driver; he was seventeen and good at it. Denise would be the navigator, charting our routes and making sure that Daniel got on the right roads. And Derek would be the treasurer; he would tell us how much we could spend on breakfast, lunch, and dinner. We had $700 in cash, and we were determined to make that see us through the entire week. The $700 came from the "family slush fund," money we saved from clipping grocery store coupons. Each week the children would cut coupons out of the paper or magazines, and when we went to the store they were in charge of using them. Whatever money we saved would go into the "jar," and everyone got to vote on how we would spend the money. Deanna, by the way, was at North Georgia College in her freshman year and could not get out to go with us, so she was going to come home and spend Easter with her father. All of our plans were taking shape.

Classes got out at noon that Wednesday before Easter, and we took off on the first leg of our trip. We drove to Washington, D.C., where I had an aunt and uncle and a cousin and his family. That first night after twelve long hours in the car we stayed with them. On Holy Thursday, we took off with lunches packed in brown bags, pockets full of change to ride the Metro, and excited spirits to be visiting our nation's capital. We did it all. We spent the whole day going from building to building and from line to line, but the children got a pretty good overall picture of what Washington was like. And everything was free, which made Derek very happy. So far the only thing we had spent money on was gas. My Aunt Ada and Uncle Tony had fed us when we arrived on Wednesday, and then their son Walt and his wife Barbara had fed us breakfast, packed our lunches, and had dinner waiting on us when we returned from our long day.

We left early Friday morning to drive to Boston where Mike and Kitty were waiting for us. The most vivid part of the trip were the toll roads from Washington all the way to Boston. Derek was going bananas at how "cheap" these states were to have toll roads. "The South is the best place in the world to live," he would utter as he logged in the expenses.

Boston seemed a long way, but we drove in and unloaded and mapped out our sightseeing plans for the next two days. The children were awed with the history: the Boston Tea Party, the Midnight Ride of Paul Revere, and Harvard. As we approached Harvard on foot, Daniel jumped in front of the statue of John Harvard, rubbed the base, and begged for knowledge. He said that this would be the closest he would ever get to Harvard. Mike and Kitty showed us every facet of Boston, and it was absolutely fascinating. We ate in great seafood restaurants, and all the while Derek was giving us our daily total of expenditures. Would we have enough to really see New York?

Easter morning came, and I called home to wish Vince and Deanna a Happy Easter. No answer. Well, I thought they must have gone to early church. I waited and called right before we sat down to lunch, and still no answer. I couldn't figure out what was going on, but I knew that Deanna would call even if Vince forgot. Late Sunday afternoon the call came from Vincent. He had been in Wrightsville and Herschel was now a Bulldog. Deanna had not come home since her father was out of town, and I got a sick feeling knowing that my daughter had stayed at college on Easter Sunday. I was lonesome for her, though she took it well, as most coaches, children do. "It was worth staying on campus if Dad finally got HIS signature on the dotted line," as Deanna stoically put it.

We left Boston on Monday with Mike and Kitty following in their car. They were going to explore New York with the Dooley gang. We had reservations at a Howard Johnson's in New York, not in the very best section of town, but not in the very worst. We could look out of our window and see people sleeping in doorways and lying on sidewalks. My children were in shock. They had never seen anything like this in their lives, and all they wanted to do was look out the window and ask a million questions.

I had tickets that first night to They're Playing Our Song. I knew the children were tired because we truly hadn't stopped since we left Athens on Wednesday, but New York was not the place to lie down and rest. We checked in, and I gave everyone one hour to be ready for dinner and then the play. Daniel rebelled: "Derek and I aren't going to any stupid play."

"You're not?" I answered. "Just what do you think you're going to do?"

"We're going to stay right here and watch TV."

"Oh no you're not," I informed him. "I haven't brought you this far to stay at the Howard Johnson's and watch TV. You can do that in Athens, Georgia. Now get that coat and tie on and be ready in forty-five minutes." He didn't argue but mumbled under his breath the whole time we were getting dressed.

Michael wanted to take them to eat at a real New York deli, so we went to one right near the theater district. Daniel was still in his rebellious mood, so he wouldn't take any advice as to what to order. He read the menu and ordered a goose liver pate sandwich. Everybody immediately challenged him with, "Daniel, do you know what you're ordering?" He assured us that he did and asked that we just leave him alone. But as any good mother would do, I said, "Daniel, you are not going to like it. You'd better change your order or you'll go hungry."

"Barbara, leave him alone," my brother advised. "He might like it, and he's certainly old enough to make food choices." The ten-dollar pate sandwich arrived. Daniel took one bite, gagged, smiled, and announced that he really wasn't very hungry. "Let the street people have it," he said. "They need it more than I do."

We arrived at the theater, the kids still teasing Daniel about his pate sandwich, and found that our seats were second row center. Awesome. Now my only hope was that the show would be good enough to keep their interest. Daniel and Derek started complaining about being at a stupid show when all they wanted to do was watch TV. Denise was excited, but the boys were really dubious about having to sit through this girl stuff . . . until it started. Then there was a transformation in my boys. Daniel was sitting on the edge of his seat with a smile as big as a jack-o-lantern, kicking his legs with the music, and Derek was in a Broadway trance. They enjoyed it so much that they begged me to get tickets to something else before we left.

New York was fun but wild. They were having a transit strike, so there were thousands of cars in the city that were not normally there. We drove to see the Statue of Liberty and the twin peaks, and it took almost three hours. It was pouring down rain, the traffic was literally bumper to bumper, and after two hours Daniel wanted to jump out and fight somebody. Daniel has a hot temper and had already wanted to fight some pothead on the street who had made an unkind remark about me. My brother grabbed his arm and told him to "just keep walking" — this was no time to prove his manhood.

We left New York after the Wednesday matinee of Peter Pan and headed toward North Carolina, where we would spend our last night on the road with Uncle Bill Dooley and his family in Chapel Hill. But right outside of New York we stopped at a motel and collapsed for the evening before heading back to the South. I don't think any of us said much except how tired we were and how happy we would be to get home. Then during the drive to North Carolina, Daniel and I had one of the biggest fights we've ever had. We were all tired and tired of each other. We needed space and we couldn't wait to get back to Athens and go to our rooms to get ourselves put back together. We got to Chapel Hill, and the Dooleys were waiting for us. Our last night on the road, and Daniel and his cousin Jim took off for a basketball game. Those two could never be around each other unless they were competing in something.

We arrived in Athens on Friday afternoon exactly eight days after we left. Derek announced that we had done it all and had thirty-five cents left in the slush fund. That would be the start of our next trip. Daniel vowed that it would be without him.

With Herschel safely in the fold, it looked like 1980 was shaping up to be a pretty good year. Herschel arrived in August, and Vince was impressed at how humble he was and how well he fit in. He did not walk around like a big man on campus, nor did he come with the attitude that he was special. He came in just as every other freshman — a little scared, full of anticipation, and looking up to the seniors. In fact, he got right into skit night and had the upperclassmen eating out of his hand from the very beginning. Herschel has always had a natural feel for public relations and dealing with people.

Our opening game that year was with Tennessee in Knoxville. We were all scared to death but so filled with excitement that I decided to go. What an evening that turned out to be! A friend from Valdosta picked some of the coaches' wives up and flew us to Knoxville. There he had two rental cars waiting, so we unloaded all of our tailgate food from the plane, loaded it in the cars, and proceeded to the campus to find a place to park and picnic before the game. The only place we could find with any parking at all was in the lot of a fast food restaurant. We stopped, all dressed in red and black, unpacked our picnic, and proceeded to party with the Tennessee folks as well as the Georgia folks. I could never eat before a game since I was so nervous, but nothing ever prevented me from talking, so I was having a grand time. I would just save my share of the food for after the game.

Tennessee kicked off, and as the teams got into the game, it looked like we didn't have a chance. They were big, they were strong, and they were playing well. At halftime the score was 15-2, Tennessee, and the Georgia fans were not too loud. We just had to win, but how? At the beginning of the third quarter Vince put Herschel in, and the electricity began to crackle not only among the players but among the fans, too. On our first TD Herschel broke three or four tackles and then stepped on their All-American safety's chest on his way into the end zone. We went wild. My thoughts immediately returned to the night I told Vince to forget Herschel—we didn't need Herschel. How happy I was that Vincent didn't listen to me and stayed after him. We won that opening game, and the

Georgia people knew that the '80s were going to be special for the Dawgs.

When we left the game, I was famished. I had played hard, and now I just wanted to eat and get home so I could see Vince and talk about the game. We went back to where the cars were parked, and they weren't there. We couldn't understand what had happened until we went inside and asked. The manager had had them towed. But we were giddy with victory, and none of us cared. They were rental cars anyway, and our host told us to just leave them and he would get us a ride to the airport. He stood out in the traffic, which was crawling, and started flagging people down asking for rides.

Finally a van stopped, and the driver told us to jump in. It was a working van and had two bench-like seats on both sides in the back — no windows. The driver was a tall, skinny man in an undershirt, jeans, flipflops, and a hat. The woman in the other seat was short and fat and wore a sleeveless sack-like dress. She had long, blond, stringy hair and looked like something left over from the flower-child years. We didn't care; we just needed a ride, and they were nice enough to stop and help. We found out that they were just passing through and happened to get caught in this ballgame traffic. They didn't even know where the airport was. Thank heavens we had driven in from the airport and knew the general direction back. When we started to unload and began thanking them, our host handed the lady a folded $100 bill. She glanced at it in the dark, quickly opened her door so the van light would come on, and yelled, "Holy Jesus. We'll take you anywhere you want to go for this." A perfect ending to a perfect game. Now if there would only be something to eat on the plane. I was starving!

At that time in our lives Derek was playing football for the youth league in Athens, and his team played on Thursday nights. Daniel played and Denise cheered for Clarke Central on Friday nights, and then the Bulldogs kicked off every Saturday, so I had a long football weekend every week during the season. Vincent was usually too busy to go to any of the children's games, but on the Thursday night before Homecoming of 1980 he said that he could come and watch Derek play. Derek was thrilled, of course, that his Dad would be there.

I can remember the first time that Vincent saw Daniel play. He was seven years old and playing for the YMCA in Athens. All of the Athens kids start out at the Y. It was the home of Fran Tarkenton, of Andy Johnson, and I just knew that it would produce another great quarterback with Daniel Dooley. I kept telling Vince how great Daniel was . . . at seven years old . . . and how he really ought to try to come watch him. One afternoon he called and said that he had to be in Jefferson, Georgia, to look at a player, but he could stop at the Y and catch a little bit of Daniel's game.

I was so excited and couldn't wait to tell Daniel that his Dad was coming to watch some of the game. As I dropped him off that afternoon I remember saying, "Do your very best; your Dad will be watching." As I look back, I see what kind of pressure that must have put on him, but he casually jumped out of the car to get ready for the game.

Vincent didn't arrive until the middle of the second quarter. The Y didn't have a stadium; it was just a series of playing fields with four different games going on at the same time. You had to know what color your child was in order to find his game. The parents either brought folding chairs or stood on the sidelines. I usually stood so I could scream and holler and tell Daniel what to do. I had even been known to get in the end zone and yell, "Come to Mama."

We were all watching the game when I felt a silence around me. I turned to see what had happened and saw Vince coming toward me. He didn't talk much, and when he entered anywhere, he tried to do it quietly, but his presence was always felt. In those days he smoked a pipe, and if you didn't hear him, you could sure smell him. He had his pipe in his mouth and stood right next to me as I informed him that it was almost halftime and Daniel was in the process of leading his team down the field to score and take the lead. Finally, it was fourth and goal with the ball on the 8-yard line. Only eight yards to go for a score. What would Daniel do? He had engineered this drive from the twenty, and we just had to score. All the parents were asking, "Wonder what play he's going to call. This is the last chance before half."

The next thing we knew Daniel had punted the ball. I was totally stunned. The sidelines were silent as death, and Vince almost bit his pipe in two. He quietly grabbed my arm — he actually pinched it — and said, "When in the hell are you going to teach your child what to do in fourth-down situations?"

"Looks like your coaching philosophy is rubbing off," I answered.

Quietly he walked over to where the team was having its halftime water break and motioned for Daniel to come to him. With his perpetual big smile Daniel eagerly ran over to talk with his Dad. He had no idea that what he had done was a bad decision. Vince put his arm around him and said, "Daniel, why on fourth down with eight yards to go for a TD did you punt? Why didn't you run or pass?" Daniel looked at him quite proudly and said, "Dad, you always told me to surprise the other team."

This particular evening in 1980, because new recruiting rules kept most head coaches in town during the week, Vincent said that he could go with me to watch Derek play. The Colts were undefeated, and Derek was cocky; even at twelve he was singing his team's praises. He and his friends never had a "pumped-up deficit," so Vincent was going to go and witness the great team in action. They did win, and after the game Derek, still in full uniform, jumped in the car with us to go home.

Vincent has never liked to just come straight home. Somewhere back in his childhood his family must have had the habit of touring around Mobile because, no matter where we go in Athens, Vincent always wants to "drag the main" before we come home. This night was especially intriguing for him because it was the Thursday before Homecoming weekend and the cheerleaders had painted a huge Bulldog head in the middle of the intersection of Clayton and College streets in downtown Athens. Plus, all of the sororities had painted the store windows with cute Homecoming themes. But it was the Bulldog head that drove Vincent to this intersection, and right as we got on top of the dog, with all three of us looking down, a drunk driver sped right through the red light and creamed us on the passenger side between the back door and the rear tire . . . right where Derek was sitting. None of us had seat belts on, and the impact flipped Derek to the ceiling of the car and to the other side. It threw me against the dash and smashed my head against the front window. It knocked Vincent against the steering wheel, busting his mouth and cutting his forehead and nose. The car spun totally around on top of the Bulldog and one back tire was found two blocks away. The car we were driving was about two days old—a shiny Lincoln Town Car that was black on the bottom and silver on top with red leather interior. I called it the "pimp-mobile."

I was raised in Catholic schools all of my life and was taught to pray every single day that when you die you will have the time and the presence of mind to pray, "Jesus, have mercy on me." I have always tried to remember that, but the last thing I remember before I was knocked unconscious was seeing the headlights coming at us and hearing the crash and thinking, "Oh crap, he's hit the pimp-mobile."

Vincent said later, "As you can probably tell, the Lord isn't ready for you yet."

Right after it happened, all I knew was that I couldn't breathe. My chest was killing me. But there was no blood anywhere on me. There were a few cuts in my head from the front window's glass but nothing major that was visible. Derek seemed fine because his helmet had protected his head and his shoulder pads, hip pads, and knee pads had protected the rest of his body. Vincent jumped out of the car bleeding profusely from the mouth—you know how lips bleed when they're cut—and there was also blood on his forehead and nose. In seconds everyone was surrounding him, asking him if he were alright. The only person who came to my side of the car was my then-neighbor and friend Joy Turnage who just happened to be outside of the movie theater talking with her teenage daughter. She ran to me, and I told her that I couldn't breathe. She quietly began praying, which gave me solace till the ambulance arrived. All the while Derek sat petrified in the back seat, repeating every minute, "Mom, are you alright? Mom, are you sure you're alright?'' We were all put in a St. Mary's ambulance and taken to the emergency room. Derek couldn't even enjoy the ride for asking me if I was alright. They checked me and found eleven broken ribs and admitted me for observation. They checked Derek and found nothing, but kept him for observation, too. Vincent, who was knocked silly and should have been kept, was able to intimidate his former-player-now-doctor, Happy Dicks, and was allowed to go home with stitches in this mouth and pills that would keep him groggy for days. In retrospect he admits that he has no recollection of the Vanderbilt game or Homecoming 1980.

The hospital was full, and the only place that they could put Derek and me was in the labor room. There was a young woman in labor who screamed all night, ''Oh Lord, help me.'' Then she would moan and scream some more. It went on like that until dawn. They had given me something that quieted me down and kept the pain from being too bad, but I never really went to sleep. I was sort of in a twilight state, feeling and hearing but not really knowing where I was. I began crying because I thought I had died and was in hell and the moaning I was hearing was all the people in hell around me begging to get out. I finally realized where I was when at dawn I heard my precious Derek say, ''Mama, are you sure you're alright?'' When I weakly responded that I was and he was not to worry about me, he said that he was hungry and could I get the nurse to bring him some breakfast. I mustered a weak smile in the knowledge that he was going to be fine. Thank God he had his uniform on!

Later that day the doctors informed me that Vincent had given them permission to operate. My spleen had been punctured and was leaking and had to come out. I couldn't believe it. Me? That was impossible. I had a speech to give in Memphis on Monday night, and Denise needed me to help her get ready for the high school Homecoming on Saturday. There was no way they were going to take my spleen out! The next thing I knew Vincent was coming to my room telling me to get tough; they had to take my spleen out. Now I knew I was going to die. I called for my parish priest. If I was going, I wanted to make sure I never heard any moaning. I wanted to go straight to Jesus with no stops along the way.

Vincent looked awful. His lips were huge with swelling and stitches, and he looked like he had been in a street brawl and lost. He stayed with me until they took me to the operating room. He knew that I was trembling on the stretcher, knew that I was fighting back tears, knew that I was thinking I would never see him or the children again. But he also knew that he had taught me to be tough, and in times of crisis I always wanted to be funny. We had through the years talked about death . . . very casually . . . and I would tease him by saying that he would be looking during my funeral service for the next Mrs. Dooley. So here I was doped up and heading down the hall on a stretcher for the operating room, and as we got to the doors, Vincent bent down to tell me that he loved me. I looked up at him and said, "Beware of women bearing casseroles." Later he admitted to being shocked that that was the last thought on my mind.

Living with a successful football coach teaches you many things, but I think one of the most important things is goal setting. Goals are like road maps that show you the destination and help you get there. You can chart your way if you know your goals. When I got home, I knew that it was going to be a slow recovery. I just hurt too much. It was October 18, and I had just about five weeks before the big Georgia-Florida game in Jacksonville. That was my first big goal, to go to that game. The doctor didn't give me much encouragement, but I knew that I would be there. I spent every day doing what it took to meet that goal.

Deanna had given her daddy a black Lab for his birthday that September, and after we beat Tennessee, we got Herschel's permission to name it in his honor. By this time, Herschel the Lab was eleven weeks old, and he laid right at my side all day long. I would struggle to get up and let him out in the yard to play, and then he would come back in and be my company. As I got stronger, I would walk in the yard with him. He loved doing that but somehow knew not to jump on me or get too rough. He helped nurse me through the lonely first weeks.

The Florida game was approaching, and Vince knew how important going to that game was to me. I had to reach my goal or I would have been mentally set back. He and the doctors talked about it and agreed that the only way I could in fact make the trip was to have a mobile home in the parking lot that I could go to if I were too weak to last the whole game. The Jacksonville Bulldog Club got the job done and had a beautiful mobile home waiting right outside of Gate 9 just in case I felt the need.

If you have never been to a Georgia-Florida game, it's almost indescribable. It's wild. It's masses of crazy people, half of them dressed in orange and blue and half dressed in red and black. The liquor flows freely from Wednesday before the game until kickoff, and some slip it in during the game. For years it has been known as "the world's largest outdoor cocktail party." Everyone tries to scream for his team louder and more obnoxiously than the next person. There are picnics and tailgates all over the parking lots, and at Wolfson Field — a baseball field right next to the Gator Bowl — the Florida Bulldog Club hosts a picnic for our coaches' wives, friends, and families. The whole affair is steeped in tradition and is the most fun and festive football game of the season. It's almost like a mini-bowl game.

I got to the pregame picnic with the help of my brother John and his wife Elaine, but when I tried to get in the gate, I knew I was in for trouble. My ribs were still sore, and people were shoving and pushing. I was still too thin and weak, but I did make it to my seat. After about five minutes the man behind me jabbed his knee into my back, accidentally of course. The pain shot to my head, and I knew that I had to get out of that crazy stadium. Johnny took me to the trailer, got me situated, and went back to our seats.

But the game was looking bleak. It really looked like Florida was getting ready to give us our first defeat of the season. How could we come this far and let Florida beat us? The minutes were ticking away; Florida had possession of the ball, and all they had to do was make a first down and the game would be theirs. Johnny barged into the trailer madder than a bunch of swarming hornets. "Your husband has cost us the game," he fumed. "I have just witnessed some of the dumbest calls that I have ever seen in my life."

I was in no mood to listen to him criticize my husband. I could do that, but nobody else had that privilege. Calmly I said, "Johnny, there is a way." I had watched the whole game on the TV in the mobile home, and I truly had not given up hope. If there was a way for Florida to screw up a game, I knew they would find it. Johnny went to the back of the trailer and looked out the window while I gave him the play-by-play. Florida had punted to us, and it was now fourth down with one minute on the clock and the Dogs backed up to their own 8-yard line. Then, out of the blue, the miracle happens. Buck Belue escapes a couple of tacklers and throws a little curl pass to Lindsey Scott that should have been good for about ten yards, but all of a sudden Lindsey is streaking down the sideline for a 79-yard winning touchdown.

I remember standing up to hug Johnny's neck and hearing him say what a great coach Vincent was. Then I looked out of the trailer window and saw a Florida man who had left the stadium thinking that they had won the game but still listening to the last minute on his portable radio. I was watching just in time to see him hurl his radio across the parking lot. Georgia had done it again, and we were undefeated going into the Auburn game. Only one more win and we would have another conference title, and then beating Tech would give us the state title. I never even thought about a national title. A national championship for Georgia? Why, impossible. Unheard of.

The next week we played Auburn at Auburn, and that was a game that I didn't go to. I had only been to Auburn once since we had left, and we lost that game. I decided never to go back. It just hurt too much! After the Auburn game we were 10 and 0, and only Georgia Tech was keeping us from an undefeated season. That game was two weeks away, which would give us plenty of time to prepare for Tech, our biggest rival.

During these two weeks, trouble was coming out of Auburn. They were going to fire their coach, Doug Barfield, and speculation ran wild. Would they really fire him after the Alabama-Auburn game, and if they did, who would replace him? We began getting calls from Auburn people wanting Vince to "come home." He would not discuss it or answer any of the calls. All that was on his mind was Wrecking Tech, and that we did, which gave us our first-ever perfect season.

The minute the Tech game was over, Auburn officially came after Vince. His alma mater was calling, and they would make it worth his while to come. Vince was not the kind of coach who went looking for jobs just to get a raise. In fact, he only seriously considered one other coaching job in his twenty-five years at Georgia, and that was after his second year here when Oklahoma offered him a job. He almost took that one, but Deanna, who was five at the time, told him she didn't want to live with the Indians. I don't think that really had anything to do with it, but he maintains that she made up his mind.

He seriously looked at the Auburn job, and I honestly thought he was going to take it. I have never been one to tell him what to do career-wise because I've always felt that he was the one who had to go to work every day. He needed to be exactly where he wanted to be. I could adjust anywhere, though I really didn't want to. The older children weren't too upset that he was thinking about leaving. In fact, I think they thought it was exciting and might be fun, but Derek, our youngest, was visibly crushed. He was ten, and the Georgia Bulldogs were his life. He couldn't imagine going to another school. Vince asked him what his thoughts were and he said, "I can't believe that you would go to AUBURN. I can't stand AUBURN!" and with that he proceeded to cry. It broke my heart.

Vince later looked at me and said, "What do you think?"

"I think that you should go where you are going to be the happiest," I told him. "You can stay here and know that you will never get another job offer and plan on retiring in Athens, or you can go to Auburn and start all over. Whatever you decide, I just want you to know that it's only a four hour drive and you can visit us on your off weekends."

I knew that going back would never be the same. We have wonderful memories of his first job, of our years as students, of meeting and falling in love . . . great memories of courting in the library, walking the campus, spending hours talking, and just getting to know each other . . . memories of our first home and the birthing of our first two children, of learning how to grill outside . . . wonderful, wonderful memories. But I knew that you can never really go back. It's never the same. It's like a child who cuts the cord of home and always wants to go back, but once there realizes it's not quite like he remembered.

I knew the Auburn people wanted a savior, and I wasn't sure Vince was up to that at this stage in his career. I had watched Johnny Majors "go home" to Tennessee and for years suffer the abuse from alums. I had watched Doug Dickey go home to Florida and subsequently get fired. I didn't want grief, and I didn't want to be a statistic. Actually, I was confident that if Vince said yes to Auburn, he would build a championship team, but I was selfish and didn't want my life disrupted. Plus, orange is not my color and I was too old to learn so many new names!

Later that night Vince walked through our den where he had all of his special players' pictures hanging. These were young men he had coached who had made All-American, All-SEC, All-Scholastic, or had just been outstanding in some way. He sat down and looked at them and for a long time didn't say a word. He finally looked at me and said, "This is what coaching is all about—coaching these young men and being a part of their lives and watching them come back year after year as productive citizens. These are our roots now, and I can't leave them." I broke down and cried. He had made his decision, and we were all going to get to stay at home.

Earlier that day our yard man, whom we had had for ten years, came to the door and asked to speak to the coach. I should mention that back in 1970 Henry had shown up out of nowhere and said, "I'm a preacher, I do yard work, and the Lord told me you needed someone to help you." He listed a few people that he worked for, and I told him that the Lord was right, I did need him, and for the next ten years he was at my door each week without fail. Now it was 1980, Vince was about to make the biggest decision of his life, and Henry wanted to talk with him. So I summoned my husband to the front door.

"Coach," said Henry, looking Vince over, "the Lord told me that you should go to Auburn."

I flipped and said, "Henry, what are you talking about?" I always jump in on conversations that interest me, and this one certainly did.

"You heard me," Henry said. "The Lord done told me that the coach should go to Auburn."

Vince saw the look on my face and in a gentle voice said, "Henry, I'm going to pray about it tonight, and tomorrow morning I'm going to have the press conference here at the house. You come on over for breakfast, and we'll see what the Lord tells me during the night."

That was quite agreeable to Henry, and he left us with the assurance that he would be back in the morning. The next day there he was in his dark blue, three-piece Sunday preaching suit with the chain of his pocket watch hooked over his vest. He looked dapper and ready for the press conference. He had breakfast with everyone, and the last I saw of him, he was having a second cup of coffee while we were setting up for the radio and TV crews.

Vince made the announcement that he was staying, and everyone was thrilled. It was a hectic morning, and I really didn't think any more about Henry. He was due to come to work the next week, and I would be able to talk to him then. But he never came back. I couldn't figure it out. He had never missed a day in ten years, and after the second week I knew something must be wrong and I started searching for him. Henry never had a telephone because he said us women would drive him crazy, so when you wanted him you had to go looking. I finally saw him after another week and said, "Henry, where have you been? I haven't seen you since the press conference, and the yard is in terrible shape."

He gave me a strange look and said, "I ain't working for anybody that don't listen to the Lord."

He didn't come back for nine years. Finally, two years ago I was walking down the street one afternoon and saw him and stopped. "Henry," I told him, "I miss you and we need you, and I've been praying that you would come back."

He smiled and said, "I reckon I can come now. I'll be there Friday." When he came that Friday, it was like he had never missed a day, let alone nine years.

Once Vince made the decision to stay, we began to realize the scars that had formed during this period of uncertainty. The coaches on our staff had begun to divide up and take sides over who would take over. Some were immediately pledging their loyalty to Erk Russell, and others were backing off and just waiting to see what would happen. Personally, I don't think Erk would have ever taken the chance at Georgia Southern if it hadn't been for this experience, because it made him realize that he really did want to be a head coach and have his own program. The other problem that Vince came back to was that he was about to play for the national championship, and some people felt that he had disrupted his team with all the talk about leaving. So now he couldn't help feeling that if he did lose, it would be blamed on his looking at the Auburn job.

People never cease to amaze me, and during this job crisis it became evident that some of our "loyal" fans were mostly loyal to themselves. I got some of the strangest calls. One lady called to say that if we did leave, would I please let her have first shot at my red and black Oriental rug. She had admired it for years and knew I would have no use for it at Auburn. Another called to say she hoped we wouldn't leave, but if we did, could she please have our Christmas wreath. Still another called to say that she loved us, but we had to go to bat for Erk and she had to have my Bulldog jewelry. I felt as though I were dying and people were casting lots for everything we had. Football fans are a rare breed; that's for sure.

Now that we had won the conference, beaten Tech, and decided to stay at Georgia, we could have Christmas and get on with the Sugar Bowl and our date with Notre Dame. Just the name Notre Dame was awesome to a Catholic family, and here we were playing them for the national championship. Vincent got letters from nuns and priests all over the country asking for tickets. Some even said, "You know we love you and have pulled for you all these years, but this is one time that we can't go against the Blessed Mother. We have to pull for Notre Dame, but could you please send us four tickets?" It got to be a joke in our family, but we were so elated with the season — winning the conference, beating our archrival Georgia Tech, and now going to New Orleans — that nothing could really spoil it. I even said to Vince, "Don't worry about not winning. Think of the honor it is just to be here. How many teams would give it all for this opportunity?"

New Orleans is always fun, but this year was truly extra special. We left the day after Christmas and would stay until January 2. That was a long time to be at a bowl, but I can remember getting to New Orleans and thinking about savoring every moment of every day. I was glad to be alive and felt extremely blessed to have experienced a perfect football season.

I was determined to take everything in because such opportunities don't come around too often. I would get up every morning early and take a four-mile walk through the French Quarter. It was a wonderful time of day to be in the Quarter, before the hustle of the tourists and the noise of the streets. It was just me, the street sweepers, and a few all-nighters winding down their evening.

I felt like it was my town until December 30, when all of the Georgia and Notre Dame fans began arriving. The whole tempo picked up, and I began feeling like they were intruding on my privacy. I was getting uptight with the reality of the game only two days away, and the more red and black I saw the more nervous I became. What hype there is leading up to big games. I learned too late in Vince's career that the best way to cope with the pressure is to remove yourself from the atmosphere. If you don't see all of the fans, hear all the music, see grown men on their knees barking, then you won't get nervous because you can focus on something else. But there was nowhere to hide in New Orleans. The game was all around you. And it was the Big One.

We have been to a lot of bowls in the twenty-five years that we were at Georgia, and the Sugar Bowl ranks right up with the best in every way. They entertain, they are hospitable, and the parties that they stage are almost spectacular. The day before the big game, the Sugar Bowl hosted a fabulous luncheon for the coaches' wives and the wives of the officials of both schools. What made it especially fun was that the theme was "hats," and they had given all the ladies a multitude of supplies to decorate a hat with — net, lace, flowers, fruits, crepe paper, jewels, whatever you could imagine. And afterward we held a fashion show to see who had been the most creative. Deanna, who is much like her dad in many ways, inherited his competitive spirit, and when they said "prize," she was determined to win. She took the centerpiece off the table — balloons, ribbons, flowers, and all and put them on her hat. Naturally she won. It was a remarkable bonnet, I must say.

I didn't realize there were any men at the luncheon until I looked across the room and spied in the midst of three hundred women a single table with all men. I immediately asked our table hostess who the men were who were crashing our luncheon, and she informed me that they were the dignitaries from Notre Dame. I certainly couldn't let this opportunity pass. I had long heard Vince speak highly of Father Hesburg, the president of the school, so I got right up and marched over to their table and introduced myself. Father Hesburg, a tall Irishman, stood up and introduced himself and everyone else at the table. After the introductions, I looked at him and said, "Father, I'm a good Catholic girl, and I sure hope the Lord hears my prayers tomorrow, and we win the football game."

Father Hesburg cleared his throat and said, "Barbara, I don't think my God has time to worry about a football game."

"Well," I replied, "I'm sure glad He doesn't, 'cause my God does."

The next day when we beat Notre Dame I wanted to send him a telegram saying, "You'd better switch to my God," but Vince gave me a lecture on humility.

It seemed like the game itself would never be played. That was the longest week I can remember and the longest game day in history. The game was at night, and the day of January 1, 1981, lasted at least forty-eight hours. That morning we started off with Mass in our room for our whole family and all of the staff who were Catholic. Vince had been wonderful until that point, but the minute Mass was over, his game face was on, and we didn't communicate with him the rest of the day.

The only time he spoke to me that I can remember was to ask me where my tickets were. I told him, and he said that he needed them. I couldn't understand why, and he informed me that one of the higher-ups on the university faculty was upset about his tickets, so Vince volunteered mine to keep him happy. I was furious, but I knew better than to say anything. This was not the time to start a confrontation over tickets. The man came by the room, and I walked out so he could see that I was hot over his imposition. Vince gave him my four tickets for his, and he looked on the back to see where they were and decided that his were actually better than mine, so he gave them back.

The rest of the afternoon, until time to meet with his team, Vince sat alone in a small sitting room in the suite. He wasn't reading, watching TV, or talking. He was sitting and thinking, psyching himself up for every possible situation. He knew that this was his chance, and he had to be ready.

I, on the other hand, was the hostess for everyone. His sister Rosezella had driven over from Mobile with some of her children and some of his other nieces and nephews. Both of my brothers and their families were there, my sister Karen, and all of my children and their friends. I couldn't begin to think of the game. I had to take care of first things first — keeping everyone happy. I praise God for allowing me to be so naïve. I might have cracked had I really thought that we might be National Champions.

The game was wild, a real thriller. Notre Dame started it off with a mistake, and we took the lead. But it was nip and tuck the whole way, with Georgia ahead near the end and everyone praying that we could just hold on for the win. The last few minutes were so crazy that I doubt if I saw any of it. My eyes were closed, I was in the fetal position screaming to the children and all who were around me, "Just hold hands and pray to Jesus." When the clock went to zero, and I knew without a doubt that we had won, I stood there and shook as I watched the sea of red cover the field. I think every Bulldog fan at the Superdome was in shock. We had finally "been to the mountain top," and no one wanted to leave. Bodies just wanted to be there hugging and hollering, "How 'bout them Dawgs!" I didn't want to take my eyes off the field or anybody down there. I just wanted to take it all in and make the night last forever.

It was a wonderful feeling, but there's an old saying among coaches, "the highs are never as high as the lows are low," and I remembered some of the bad moments and knew it was true. I wanted this to be as high as possible. The girls and I fought our way through the sea of red to the dressing room, hugging and kissing and crying till we saw Vince. What a look he gave us—the most brilliant smile that has ever been on his face. He was ecstatically exhausted!

The minute we got back to the hotel, we were ready for the staff to come to our room to party. The game would be hashed and rehashed for many a day, but Vince liked to have his staff around him after a game, win or lose. They came, along with many other friends and relatives offering congratulations. Derek and his friend, Hamp, decided that this victory merited room service and called and ordered a prime rib meal. I almost fell out when the waiter arrived at our door with their "victory banquet," but Vince was so impressed with their initiative that he got them to order him one. And the night went on.

Finally, about one o'clock, I was exhausted and told everyone left in the room good night. We were leaving the next morning, and I just had to get some rest. I don't know when Vince finally came to bed, but early in the morning I rolled over and saw him sound asleep with all of his clothes on and his sideline pass proudly hanging from the sweater button on his chest.

He had a short night because he had to be on "The Today Show" the next morning at six, so he got up about five, showered and dressed, and left the hotel. As he was leaving, he saw our son Daniel coming into the hotel—obviously after having been out all night. Vince said good morning to him and reminded him that the bus would be leaving at nine. When Vince finished his show, he came back to the hotel and got everyone up, including Daniel. I think Daniel had been to sleep about one hour at that point, but he knew that he'd better get up and act alert.

We all packed, checked out, and were on our way home with glorious remembrances of New Orleans. Vince and I usually sit together on the plane, but this particular trip he requested the seat next to Daniel. He never said a word to Daniel about staying out all night, but he was quietly making his point. He talked to Daniel the whole way to Atlanta, and every time Daniel looked like his eyes were shutting, Vince would bring up another topic. Finally, when we got to Atlanta, he told Daniel they were all going to see Uncle Billy play in the Peach Bowl. I saw Daniel look at me like, "Do I have to?" and I promptly chimed in about how much fun they would all have. He knew that he had had it and couldn't put up any kind of argument.

Vince sat next to him at the game and kept up the chatter the whole time. Derek told me later that he had never, in all of his ten years, heard his dad talk so much. Vince kept Daniel awake until after the bowl game, and then when they all went to dinner, Daniel decided to decline and stay at the hotel and sleep. I think it was a lesson that he has never forgotten.

It had been a year of fun, of pain, of joy, and of sadness. It had brought every emotion that the human psyche could experience, and it's now a proud memory for all the Georgia people who will talk about it and savor it for years to come. It truly was the year that was!

Barbara's dad, Wallace Meshad.

Barbara and her mother, "T."

Barbara Meshad, Auburn coed.

Vince and Barbara, man and wife.

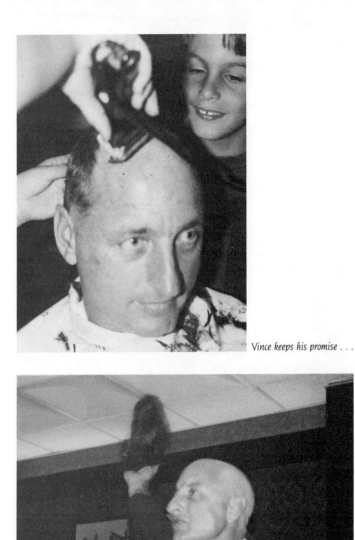

Vince keeps his promise . . .

. . . and wows the crowd at the 1976 SEC Championship banquet.

Denise, Derek, Barbara, Deanna, and Daniel.

Barbara in her "mermaid" dress, along with Vince, Betsy and Don Leebern, and Patti and Nick Chilivis.

126

The Dooley girls at Christmas: Denise, Barbara, and Deanna.

Barbara (front, center) and friends celebrate her 50th birthday.

The wedding party poses after daughter Denise's marriage.

Vince gets kiss after winning his last home game and 200th victory overall; grandson Patrick shares the moment.

OF PRESS HOUNDS AND PRIVACY

If we hadn't realized it before, winning the championship in 1980 taught us what it was like to live under a microscope.

The pressure on a coach is greater today than ever before, largely because of the relentless presence of the media. When we first got into coaching some thirty-five years ago, before Watergate and investigative journalism, the sports media were generally friendly. The men of the press (no women back then had dared break into the locker room) never set out to hurt you and most of the time printed favorable stories. If they thought you were doing a poor job, they would say so, but not with a vicious or vindictive attitude. Journalists were not to be feared or dreaded and were generally friends of football.

I can remember joking and talking with writers twenty-six years ago and never being afraid of what they might say that I said. I can also remember, at one SEC meeting, one of the head coaches had too much to drink and pushed Alf Van Hoose of the *Birmingham News* into the pool. Alf was known for wearing his glasses on his head and smoking a pipe, and the last thing we saw as he went under was the burning tobacco in the pipe and his glasses floating on top of the water. That was never reported as a sensational story, nor did the coach lose his job or self-respect.

The late coach Ralph Jordan, who was Vince's coach and employer at Auburn, had a good relationship with the press, but he despised the "poison pen" types and tried to avoid them at all costs. The SEC had a "Skywriters Tour" for many years where reporters from all over the SEC would fly from one school to the next during August practice and talk to the coaches and players. None of the coaches liked it, but it was a necessary evil. It was like the superintendent of a school system coming to visit different schools under his domain. Everyone was on his very best behavior.

Rumors were flying this particular year in the early '60s that Coach Jordan had cancer and that it was terminal. There is always one brazen reporter in every group, so after all the predictable questions had been asked, this one reporter said, "Coach Jordan, is it true that you have terminal cancer and will probably not live too much longer?" Coach Jordan replied, "Sir, you can rest assured that if I only had a few days left, I would not be spending them with you bastards."

I have had very few run-ins with reporters, but I have gone eyeball to eyeball with those that I felt were unfair in their writing about Vince. Some reporters today will stoop to any level to get a story. They invade your privacy, and they fabricate stories to try and get you to respond. They will do anything to get the scoop.

When Vince went to interview at Auburn in 1980, they surrounded our home. Vince was not even in town, but they were camped out in our yard and in our driveway anyway. If we walked out of the house, cameras and microphones were in our faces trying to get information about the situation. The children stayed away most of the day because it was so bizarre. I had threatened them about saying a word to any of the media, so they tried to avoid the whole thing. The funny thing was that we probably knew less about what was really happening than they did, and periodically I would stick my head out and ask for the latest news. I think the ultimate was when I got in the car to go to the grocery store and a TV camera followed me out of the drive to report that I was leaving. When I returned a few minutes later, that same reporter, with his cameraman behind him, opened my car door and asked what I had gotten at the store. I only wish I had had the foresight and the guts to flash a box of Tampax.

Nothing daunts the press, and my rudeness didn't faze anybody. They were after a story, and they were not leaving until they knew if Vince were taking the Auburn job. When the sun set and the children were all in, we rehashed the day's events and wondered about our fate. But one thing was for sure: we were going to circle the wagons and hold out against this invading horde.

We crawled from room to room so they wouldn't know where we were. We kept all of the lights on so they couldn't tell what we were doing. This was war and we were going to win. Then, at 11:00 p.m. on the second day of battle, the doorbell rang. The children were in bed and knew not to answer it, and I sat in the den thinking whoever it was would go away. Not so. The bell rang again. My Lebanese temper took control at that point, and when I opened the door, that obnoxious reporter probably wished an earthquake had absorbed him. I was verbally violent, I must say, and he realized that he had crossed the magic line and entered into Barbara's crazy zone. We had no further problems with reporters ringing our bell, nor have we since then.

Seems like we were always doing something that stirred the press and called for excitement. Press conferences became a yearly event for some reason or another. Our life truly changed after we won the national championship. Everything Vince did or said was news. I can remember the summer when the news broke that Vince might quit coaching and run for the senate. We were on our way to Scandinavia that July, and when we arrived at the airport to check in, the terminal was full of reporters. It made me mad that they had intruded upon my vacation time, but it really made me mad that they had whisked Vince into a room and left me to handle all of the baggage and tickets.

Vince told them that no decision would be made until our return and in fact gave them a date three weeks away. I thought that was smart. They would leave us alone for at least three weeks. Wrong! As we took our seats on the plane, I looked across the aisle, and right there before my eyes was a reporter from the *Atlanta Journal*. He was sitting right across from me! I, of course, had to say something, so I immediately asked, "What are you doing here?"

"I'm going with you," he said. "I'm sticking with you for a few days till I get a story."

Without even thinking, I asked, "How did they pick you to come with us?"

"I was the only one in the sports department with a valid passport," he answered.

This was one of the nicer reporters and one that I had always liked, but my immediate thought was, "They sure didn't pick you for your brain." He stayed right with us for five days and then returned to Atlanta without a major story. Later, he joked that at least he got a trip out of it.

Once he left, we never really thought about what was being reported in the sports section of the Atlanta paper. That was always a pleasant thing about being abroad — relief from the newspaper. It's amazing how nicely your day can start without it.

About thirty minutes before we landed back in Atlanta, one of the flight attendants came to us and said that the pilot had just been radioed that the Atlanta airport was full of reporters and cameras waiting on our arrival, and did Vince want Delta to set up a room for a press conference? What chaos we came home to. I knew for the first time how movie stars feel when they want to throw something at the camera. A thousand cameras whirred in our faces, and reporters were yelling questions as we deplaned. This time it wasn't just sports reporters but political writers, too. They whisked us into a room set up with chairs and a table for a press conference. The questions began. I should never have been there because, for the first time ever that I can remember, I was overwhelmed and couldn't even think.

I remember one political writer asking me directly whether I would rather live in Washington or on West Paces Ferry Road (the home of the governor of Georgia). I knew that he had me over a barrel and that whatever I said would be wrong. But in that situation you don't think; you just answer. And what popped out of my mouth was, "West Paces Ferry wouldn't be bad." That came back to haunt me a few years later when Vince got other political ideas, and everyone thought that I was the motive behind his political quest. I don't know why I've never learned to say, "No comment."

In 1979 we had two good quarterbacks, Buck Belue, a junior, and Jeff Pyburn, a senior. Vince used both of them, which did not make the Georgia people happy because Buck was the crowd favorite. To make matters worse, Jeff's father, Jim, was a coach on our staff, so the situation was touchy, at best. There was tension among the coaches, tension among the coaches' wives, and tension on our team.

Sports Illustrated sent a writer in to do a story on Georgia, and I happened to invite myself to lunch that day with Vince and the writer. This guy from *Sports Illustrated* seemed to be a super person, and I let my guard down and began talking to him like I would any of my friends. He started asking Vince about why he played both Buck and Jeff rather than naming one as THE quarterback. Towards dessert, when he knew I was comfortable with him, he asked if I had any influence on Vince as to whom he played. In an effort to be cute, and certainly not meaning it or even thinking, I said, "I sure do. Every night while Vince is asleep, I lean over and say, 'Buck Belue, Buck Belue.'"

He laughed, and I thought how clever I had been, until the next month when the story broke. Sure enough, he had quoted me as plugging Buck over my longtime close friends, the Pyburns. After that season Jim left coaching, and it was years before Ann would speak to me again. I sure learned a weighty lesson on that one. It's one thing to be cute and clever, but it's another thing to run your mouth in front of a reporter at someone else's expense.

Herschel Walker was the most recruited player in the world, and he certainly changed our lives. We went from relative obscurity to national prominence and what was to become a decade of rollercoaster ups and downs. We had the press now, and they would always be with us in a big way. Our sports information director, Claude Felton, came to us in 1979, and by Vince's retirement in 1988 he had arranged every kind of press conference you could imagine. He would shake his head at every crisis and say, "I can't believe this is happening." I used to tease him and tell him he could hire out as a freelance press conferences coordinator.

The media really had a field day with the Jan Kemp scandal. They were determined that Vince was guilty of something, and they were out to prove their theory. That period of Georgia football probably caused Vince to lose his enthusiasm for the job more than any other single episode.

When the Kemp story broke, we actually thought it was a joke. At first, no one took her seriously because we knew that most of what she was charging was not true. She had some legitimate concerns but no way to properly express her grievances. She did not have any complaints with Vince, but because she could not get our president to listen to her, she took the university to court over a First Amendment violation after she was fired. Because some of her complaints centered around preferential treatment of athletes, the story drew national media attention.

The school's attorney fumbled the ball on the opening kick when he said, in effect, that it was alright to keep the athletes in school if we could "raise them from the garbage truck to the post office." I could not believe he made that statement. It set the tone for a flamboyant, often exaggerated trial that the press just couldn't get enough of. Jan Kemp won her case mainly in the newspapers.

Having your life and work subjected to constant public scrutiny is simply not easy, and it may be harder on a coach's family members than on the coach himself. I can remember so vividly when Daniel was a little boy playing for the YMCA and Vince had two very mediocre seasons. The fans were not happy; in fact, some students actually hanged him in effigy. I got really upset, but he calmly remarked that he must have finally made it as a head coach now that he had been hanged in effigy!

Anyway, Daniel would go to the YMCA, and his little friends would parrot what they had heard their parents say. One boy said, "Your dad is the dumbest coach we have ever had." That was all it took. Daniel beat him up. When I picked up the carpool that afternoon, the boy Daniel had beat up was one of the kids in my car. I immediately knew something was wrong because all the boys were too quiet. I said, "What's happened, Daniel?"

"Mama, it's nothing," he said. "I was just helping a friend understand football."

I did not ask any more questions at the time, but to this day they are still friends, and I believe Daniel's attitude reflected a lot of his daddy's burden.

One of my most vivid recollections of the press happened years ago when we were at the Tangerine Bowl in the mid-seventies. One of Orlando's leading lady journalists called and asked me for an interview for the social section of the Orlando paper. I told her that I would love to meet her, and we set a time to meet in the lobby of the hotel. I arrived a few minutes before her, and when she came in, I heard her ask the desk for my room. I immediately went over and introduced myself to her. She looked at me and said, "You can't be Barbara Dooley, you're a foreigner."

For a second I was taken aback, but I gathered my wits and said, "I am Barbara Dooley. Coach Dooley just believed in integration long before the Civil Rights Bill in 1964."

I couldn't believe that this woman had been so callous and hurt my feelings, but I went on with the interview as if nothing had happened. I have never once thought of myself as a foreigner, but for the first time in my life I felt the sting of discrimination, and knew that I would never — or ever want to — harbor discriminatory thoughts.

Television is something that truly scares me. I have never felt really comfortable in front of a camera because once you've said it you can't take it back. If you cross your legs wrong, it's there for everyone to see. Television just makes you too vulnerable, and I don't like for everyone to see my mistakes. But Vince has done a lot of television and had agreed to an interview with a station in Atlanta. They asked if they could do it at our home so that people could see the family side of Vince Dooley. They also asked if I would be in the interview. Vince promptly replied that if they were going to include me, he would never get a word in.

But they wanted me in the interview, so it was set. They had us sitting on our sofa in the den, and it was to be just a casual, at-home kind of talk. Bill Hartman, the channel's sportscaster and our longtime friend, was doing the interview, and he asked, "Barbara, now that all of the children are gone what do you two do with yourselves?" First of all, that was a question I didn't expect, and I really didn't have an answer prepared, so right off the top of my head I said, "Oh, the minute he comes home now, I just throw him on the couch and start making passionate love." I thought Vince was going to fall out, and Bill Hartman did. But he aired it, and all the men in the state thought Vince was their new hero!

Bill Hartman brings out the devilment in me, maybe because I've known him for so long, but I seem to do the worst things when he's involved in an interview. After Vince retired, the biggest event of the fall was following him to the first football game as a spectator and fan. It was Ray Goff's kickoff as Georgia's head coach, and it was a super hype. I knew Bill was going to film Vince sitting in the box and watching the game, but I never saw them wire Vince up for sound, nor did I see that small microphone on Vince's tie. All I was told was to sit down next to Vince during the game so they could get some shots. I did as I was told.

The excitement was building, and everyone was waiting for the kickoff. They played "The Star Spangled Banner." They said the prayer, and then everyone began to go, "Woof, woof," yelling for the kickoff. Finally, the whistle blew, the camera started rolling, and the big moment for Ray Goff arrived — his first kickoff as Georgia's head coach. The minute the ball got into the air, I leaned over to Vince and whispered — unknowingly — right into his microphone, "Don't you know that Ray has just crapped in his pants?"

The TV cameraman fell over backwards, and I saw Vince point to the microphone on his tie. Vince had always said, "If she thinks it, she says it." I really don't understand why I don't have more self-control, but I don't, and it doesn't seem to get any better with age.

But seriously, the big problem that I see with the media is that in their efforts to tell, or get, a story they won't leave you alone to make your decisions. Media attention just builds the pressure, and any kind of news becomes a crisis in your life. People you don't even know become part of your decision-making process. I have often asked retired coaches what they like most about not coaching, and every one of them has said, "I don't ever have to deal with the press again." Vince had always treated the press with respect, as he would want to be treated. They have not always responded in kind.

EMPTYING THE NEST

As much as we talk about it and plan for it, I'm not sure any parent is ever really ready to see his or her children leave home for college. It's not that you don't want them to go, but you know that this is really a milestone in your life as well as theirs. You also know that as much as you love them and they love you, your relationship will never be the same. Maybe it will improve and grow into a relationship better than you can imagine, but few of us really enjoy taking such chances.

I can remember so vividly when my daddy took me to Auburn for my first day of college. Our car was loaded with everything I owned, which I thought was a lot until years later when I saw what my children left with. Mother and I had said our goodbyes earlier, and as we were backing out of the driveway, I saw her pretending to be weeding her plants while sobbing. I didn't understand why she would be crying. Going off to school was the happiest day of my life. I turned to Daddy and said in amazement, "Why is Mother crying because I'm going to Auburn? She acts like

I'm dying or something."

Daddy, who was a big Alabama fan, said, "Well, going to Auburn is like dying. In fact, I'm not so sure she would take your death this hard."

My daddy the clown! He was hurting too, but I wouldn't understand for twenty-five years.

I had spent the whole summer getting Deanna ready to go to North Georgia College. We had met with her roommate and decided on colors for bedspreads, colors for towels and sheets, who was bringing the stereo, who was bringing the TV, who was bringing the refrigerator. Of course, there was never mention of a typewriter, a desk light, a wastebasket, or anything related to school or learning. Finally, after sounding like some stranger from another planet, I decided to shut up and let her plan her college room. What she didn't bring she could come home and get. She would only be two hours away. We had her sheets and towels monogrammed. We had new everything. Everything had to be perfect. We couldn't go to college with anything that might resemble Salvation Army Used.

She decided that everything we had all shared was now hers. The blouses that she and Denise both wore were hers to take. The sweaters were hers. After many arguments over what was hers and what was ours, I told Denise to let her take it all. We'd just go out and get new replacements, and that would really do her in when she came home and saw all of our new clothes.

Any of you who have girls close in age know the perils of sharing clothes. They have had countless fights through the years over what was whose. One morning after an argument over a blouse, I called them both in my room and told them that none of us owned anything solely. We were a family, and that meant everything we had was shared. I would share and they would share. I never wanted to hear any more words over something being "mine." I thought that I had come up with a brilliant plan until a week later. I looked for my new silk blouse and couldn't find it. After looking diligently again, I went upstairs and found it on the floor under Denise's bed. I was furious. First of all, it was brand new. Second, it was the most money that I had ever spent on a blouse. And third, it was mine! I couldn't believe it was on the floor, under her bed, and all wadded up. I moped all day about the blouse, and when Denise came home from school, I attacked her. Her response was "You said everything was OURS, and I just thought what a great blouse WE had bought." I set some new ground rules after that.

The day finally arrived for Deanna to go to school. She had spent two weeks packing, and the whole family was ready for her to leave. We had enough chicken boxes from the grocery store to fill a warehouse, and she was organizing each one of them. Daniel and Derek loaded the car, and she bade her farewells to Denise, Daniel, and her dad. His last words were, "I expect you to do your best in everything that you do and remember what you are up there for."

Derek was going with me. He wanted to see the campus, and he would help us unload. By the time we got halfway there, I began choking up. It was now becoming a reality — one I thought I had prepared myself for but hadn't. This was going to be tough — taking my oldest baby to school and just leaving her there. I was so glad that Derek was with me because he was as full of anticipation as she was, and they talked the entire trip.

We arrived, found her dorm, and began unloading. If you are ever sad about seeing them go, you are mad by the time you unload a car in the heat of August and climb stairs to fix a dorm room. I thought we would never get finished, and the only thing that saved us was that her roommate's father was there to do all of the heavy carrying and complicated fixing. Finally, we got her settled, and it was time to say goodbye when I remembered that I hadn't bought her anything for her refrigerator. I, who screamed every time the girls put a calorie in their mouths, was suggesting a trip to the corner store to get her some snacks. Of course, she jumped on that idea, and off we went to get everything she wanted. She said later that she knew I was sad when I started throwing Snickers bars and Oreo cookies in her basket. Denise would never believe that story!

I had dallied too long; there was nothing else to keep me there. I had to tell her goodbye, and when I did, I started crying and so did she. She got out of the car crying, and I sobbed all the way back to Athens. Poor Derek, he felt bad, too, but he just couldn't understand why I was taking it so hard. I cried every day for two weeks, and then we settled into family life minus Deanna. I have often told my friends that you cry when they leave and then you cry when you see them come home for the summer with all the junk that left your house in the fall.

Children are all different, and ours are no exception. Two years later, when Daniel and Denise left, it was nothing like Deanna's departure. They were really ready to leave, and I was ready for them to go. Their senior year of high school had just about finished me off. I am convinced that the Lord helps you cut the cord with most of your children because they get so wild and ready to be on their own that last year of high school, you are ready to send them early!

Daniel played football all through grammar school, was on the state championship team in high school, and decided, even though he had terrible knees, that he was going to Georgia and "walk on" and play for his dad. I was not going to allow it. I wanted him to go to Valdosta State and play ball there, where he would have a chance to be successful and be his own man. I didn't think that he needed to prove himself at Georgia. I felt there would be too much pressure on him as the coach's son and too much pressure on Vince, coaching his own son. But he wouldn't listen to me.

That spring on our family trip out West, he sat next to Vince on the plane and convinced him that he ought to go to Georgia to play football. I didn't know any of this had taken place until we got home and one morning over breakfast Daniel informed me that his dad had said it was alright for him to go to Georgia. This was so unlike Vince. We had always stuck together on decisions, and if one didn't agree with the other, we would talk it out until we both agreed. But he had never discussed this issue with me and had given Daniel permission to go to Georgia. I was furious and told him so. He, in turn, was shocked because he didn't know that I had told Daniel that I didn't think it was best for him to come to Georgia. Daniel hadn't told Vince that we had discussed it. But the decision had been made, and Vince was going to let Daniel come to Georgia.

As the days went by, I think he began to regret letting Daniel talk him into it, so every morning at breakfast he would have a new rule for him. First it was, "Daniel, if you come to Georgia, you can't bring your dirty clothes home for your mother to wash." The next morning he said, "Daniel, if you come to Georgia, don't think you are going to come home and eat.'' The third morning he said, ''Daniel, if you come to Georgia, don't think you're going to bring your friends over here and make this the hangout.''

Finally I couldn't take it anymore. I exploded.

''You've given him permission to go to Georgia against my will,'' I fumed, ''and now you're trying to run my son away from me. He can do anything he wants. He can bring his clothes home, he can eat here anytime he wants to, and he can bring anyone he wants to home with him.'' With that I got up from the table crying and went to my room and slammed the door.

A minute later my flew door open, and in stormed Vincent. He looked at me and said, ''There's only one thing worse than having a walk-on for a son, and that's sleeping with a walk-on's mother.''

I went to Atlanta one August day to back-to-school shop with Denise, and when I got home, Daniel had moved into the football dormitory. He left me a note that said, ''Mom, I'm gone. I've got everything. I love you. Daniel.'' I couldn't believe that was how he went to school. No fanfare, no new towels — in fact, he took the oldest things we had — but most of all, no goodbyes. He didn't want to see me fall apart. He was determined to be his own person, and for weeks I didn't see him or hear from him. I would get reports from Vince on him, and I knew that he was okay, but I couldn't understand why he wouldn't come home or call. Later he told me that he had to do it that way so that none of the boys would think that he was the kind of person who would run home to Mama. He had to prove that he was as macho as the next, but he confessed that many a night he seriously considered coming home, especially during freshman initiation.

By the time he was a junior in college he was a little more comfortable about coming home and bringing some of the football players when his dad was out of town. They would never come over here if they thought Coach Dooley might come home. Daniel's birthday is in March, and I told him that I would like for him to invite a few of his friends over for dinner to celebrate. His Dad would be out of town and they could have a party over here. He invited some of his closest friends and their dates and assured them that his Dad would be out of town. They were all of age, and I didn't think one thing wrong with serving them a beer before dinner.

As they were sitting in the den laughing and telling football stories Vince unexpectedly drove up. The weather was awful, and his plane couldn't take off. Before I could warn them, he was in the back shaking hands and telling them hello. They wanted to eat those beer cans, but there was nowhere to hide them. Finally, Vince walked out of the room, and they tried to gather their composure. It was one thing to be in the head coach's house, but to be there with a can of beer was the ultimate. I knew the party was over and they would not be able to eat a bite, but what could I say?

About five minutes later Vince solved the dilemma by going in the back and telling Daniel that the gutter was stopped up and he needed him to get up there and clean it out so the rainwater would have a place to go. Daniel was all dressed up in his new pants and sweater, but he didn't protest. With all of his friends and their dates looking out the window laughing, Daniel climbed on the roof in the pouring rain and cleaned out the gutter. I quickly cleaned up all evidence of beer, poured some tea, and we all sat down to a fun birthday dinner. I bet the boys will be telling this one to their grandchildren.

Daniel Dooley has always been tough. He has always had a tough heart, and he's got a pretty mean streak that you don't see often, but when he competes he wants to win. And I knew when he walked on at the University of Georgia, he was going to give it all he had and go for the gold. But I also knew that he would be under a lot of pressure to perform for his father, and that worried me.

I used to joke that when kids go off to school they only call you for two reasons: when they're out of money or when they're stressed. They tell you all their horror stories and get you feeling so sorry for them, and then they hang up and go out and party while you brood all night over how miserable they are. But Daniel would call me after a particularly bad practice and tell me how rough it was or how mean the coaches were or how they were really picking on him. The minute Vince walked in for dinner I would say, "Vincent, why did Coach So-and-so jump on Daniel? He's picking on him and I'll tell you what: if he doesn't leave him alone, I'm going to confront him." Vince listened to me and listened to me and kept saying, "This is why I didn't want my son at Georgia; I knew you were going to try to interfere." I never really did interfere, but I used to let Daniel and Vince think I was going to.

Finally, Daniel called me one night in the pits of depression and said, "Mom, I've really done it this time. I really think Dad might kick me off of the team."

"Daniel," I said, "what in the world have you done?"

"Well," he answered, "today at practice they were on my back for everything. Coach Lewis would scream at me, and then Coach Cavin would scream at me. It was always somebody screaming Dooley this and Dooley that. I wasn't doing a thing right. Finally, I decided I was going to show them." He said that his job that day was holding the blocking dummy while everybody had to come hit it, and all of a sudden he saw Herschel running as fast as he could toward the thing. He said, "When I saw Herschel coming, I just thought, 'I'm going to stick it to him.'" Well, there was an unspoken rule at practice that you didn't stick anything to Herschel, especially a blocking dummy. You let Herschel hit it at the speed he wanted to hit it.

But Daniel was bowed up, and he wanted to show the coaches that he was giving it his best. So when Herschel hit the blocking dummy, Daniel jabbed it to him. And before Herschel had time to bounce off, Coach Cavin had his hand around Daniel's neck and his finger pointing between his eyes, saying, "Son, you do that again and I'm going to tell your daddy, and we're going to ship your tail to Iran."

After two years of giving it all he had, and after having his third knee operation, Daniel had to give up football. He became a manager for the last two years he was in college. He enjoyed that, but you could tell his heart was broken that he never really got to play for the University of Georgia.

By the time I took Denise to Valdosta State a few weeks later, I was really feeling the effects of going from a full house to only one child. It was sad. My life was really going to change, and not slowly. I was in the jolt mode. I had not recovered from Daniel leaving, and here I found myself kissing Denise goodbye. This time I was going it alone because Derek was in football practice and couldn't leave and so was Vince. I cried all the way home, but when I got there, Derek was just waiting to tell me how great it was going to be having the house all to himself and not having to share anything with anybody.

We did go from a loud, noisy house to a very quiet one immediately. Derek would leave the house with Vince at seven in the morning, and he wouldn't come home until seven-thirty that night. He would eat dinner, study, and fall into bed. There was very little conversation during football season. Vince never came home before eleven, so I found myself with many hours to fill, but it didn't take me long to enjoy my new-found freedom. It was the first time in years that I actually had time for myself, and it was wonderful. If this was the empty-nest syndrome, I was pretty sure I could handle it.

I remember so vividly that first Thanksgiving when all of the children came home for the holidays. The noise level got back up there, and I was a wreck by the time they all left on Sunday. After everybody had gone, Derek came into my room and said, "Mama, I love Deanna and Daniel and Denise, but I'm sure glad they've gone back and we can get back to normal." He loved being the only child and made no bones about it. It was funny when they all came home and we would gather in the kitchen and talk. Guess who would be the loudest. None other than Derek. When we were in the house by ourselves, he might go a week without talking, but when the older three wanted my attention, he jumped right in full steam ahead.

Derek and I spent four years together without the other children being home, and we were really close. Vince was always at work, so Derek really was my only companion when we were at home. He had loads of friends and went out a lot, but when he was at home we had plenty of quality time together. In fact, every night before we went to bed he would come in my room and crawl in bed with me and discuss the day or whatever was on his mind. I knew that when he left for college I was going to fall apart, but I wasn't going to think about it until I absolutely had to.

HAPPY HOLIDAYS

I can only remember maybe five New Year's Eves being fun in the twenty-five years that Vince was Georgia's head coach. Three things could happen: one, we wouldn't go to a bowl; two, we would go to a bowl early before New Year's Eve and lose it, which would make Vince miserable through the whole New Year's Eve and New Year's Day holiday. Or three, we would play in a New Year's Day bowl, and Vince would be all uptight during New Year's Eve and totally focused on the football game the next day. As much as he tried to be pleasant, there really was just no way.

Vince's characteristic New Year's Eve behavior was on display the night before the national championship game. The Sugar Bowl puts on a big, elegant dinner dance. Tradition has it that after dinner the two head coaches ceremonially light the creme brulee dessert before the waiters served it, so this was a special affair for us.

It was a truly fabulous black-tie occasion, and I had purchased a wonderful dress. It was silver with sequins from the top of the jeweled neckline to the floor. It had steel-gray flounces that ran down the sides and around to the back. It looked like a mermaid dress. It was flashy and it was different. When I put it on, I knew it was a wonderful dress; I also knew that it was very unusual, and I always love to judge women's reactions to what I have on. I always tell Vince what I think certain people are going to say and then wait to see if I was right.

Some women are interesting in that, if another woman intimidates them by the way she dresses, they will give her a backhanded compliment; they'll make a negative comment in a positive way. This particular lady I knew was a master at this, and I knew she was going to be the first to approach me and comment on my dress. Sure enough, before I got in the door good, she walked up to me, with Vince standing right there on my arm, and said, "Oh my gosh, you look absolutely wonderful. You look just like a fish."

I wanted to say, "I'm sorry I'm not a shark so I could annihilate you," but I didn't. I smiled and thanked her like I was too dumb to know what she was doing and nudged Vince like I told him so.

The point is, Vince was right there watching, presumably listening, presumably feeling my elbow in his side, but he has absolutely no memory of it. His mind was so focused on the game the next day that he might as well not have been there.

What's more, as soon as he performed his official act of lighting the dessert, we left. I couldn't believe that we had gotten all dressed up for thirty minutes, but he wasn't about to party and enjoy himself the night before the game. His offered his usual statement (which makes me absolutely furious): "You can stay, but I'm leaving."

And some years it wasn't just New Year's that was ruined. I can remember one of the worst moods he has ever been in was after we had played in Tampa in the Hall of Fame Bowl in 1984. The game was played on December 23, and we were all coming home on December 24, which in itself was a nightmare. Traditionally we opened presents, cooked the big meal, and did everything on the 24th, and the kids didn't want to change the routine. So when we got to Atlanta at about noon, I would have to go home after being gone a week, get at least five loads of clothes in the wash, run to the grocery store and pick up enough food to cook the big meal that night, get it on the table, and then act like it was fun to open presents that night. But in order to keep traditions alive, I was going to give it my best shot.

We lost the football game and Vince Dooley was miserable. He was a total Scrooge. In fact, we were all calling him Scrooge behind his back, but only behind his back. When he has lost and is upset, I have learned to tread softly. I babied him all the way back on the plane, didn't talk too much, spoke only when spoken to, ignored him when that seemed best, and went about my business with the children. I kept feeling that the longer we waited and left him alone, the longer he would have to sort out his feelings and get to feeling better. It was the holiday, the children were in college and we didn't see them often, and I wanted it to be happy. My attitude was we had played the game, we had lost, it was over, and what good was moping. Now we needed to get on with Christmas.

We flew home, landed in Atlanta, and then boarded the charter buses for the ride back to Athens. We finally got home around two and unloaded the car, and I don't even think Vince even came in. He went straight to the office.

It was Christmas Eve, and the girls pitched in so that we could have Christmas dinner that evening. It had to be a team effort to pull it off, but we did. I had set the table before we ever left for Tampa, so that part was done, though the dishes had gathered a little dust. I had made a couple of casseroles that just needed pulling out of the freezer. I threw together a few of their favorite dishes that didn't take a lot of time, pulled the smoked turkey out, and we were ready for Christmas Eve by seven-thirty that night.

We were all in a festive mood. Christmas music was playing in the house, and all of the kids were scurrying around getting their last-minute presents under the tree. We were all happily anticipating just being together and opening presents. Vincent came in and tried really hard to be nice, but he just couldn't muster any enthusiasm for the season. He had gotten beat, and he was miserable, and it was going to be a long winter.

We ate dinner laughing and talking, and Vince never participated. He went to the back den with us to open presents, but he was just going through the motions. He was emotionally not with us, and he certainly wasn't with us mentally. We sat around and opened presents and screamed, "Oh, we love this," and "This is wonderful," and "This is just what I want"—all the normal exclamations of pleasure. Daniel always writes poems with his gifts, and it's the highlight of Christmas to hear his poetry to the family. So we were listening and laughing, and Vince would speak every once in awhile but not often. He would open a gift, glance at it, and just put it down—no emotion, no gratitude, and absolutely no Christmas spirit.

I was getting madder and madder. There are times when I get really tired of football totally dominating our lives, and this was one of those times. It just seems to me that you can turn some things off. But he couldn't. He hates to lose, and it affected his whole person. His attitude was shot, and he couldn't pull himself out of it.

The kids were all coming to me quietly and saying, "Mama, what's wrong with him? He's awful. He's a Scrooge. He can't even enjoy Christmas."

"Well," I said, "I'll tell you what. I'll bet you tomorrow, on Christmas Day, after he's had a good night's sleep, he'll get into the swing of things."

The next morning was no better. He took his shower and dressed for Christmas Mass and morosely proceeded to take us to church. He was still not with us. Deanna and her husband, Lindsey, had left to go to Colquitt, Georgia, and be with his parents on Christmas Day since we had celebrated the night before. Daniel, Denise, and Derek were with us at Mass, and then I had invited them to come back to the house for sandwiches — leftover turkey sandwiches, which suited me fine. I was tired and really couldn't go through another big meal. I think it suited everybody fine, so we went home after Mass, and everybody changed into their grub clothes just to hang out and enjoy Christmas afternoon as a family.

We were all sitting around the chopping block in the kitchen laughing and talking when Vince walked in for lunch. He took his place at the chopping block, put both hands under his chin, and sat there propped on his elbows with the faraway, miserable, moping look that I had been looking at for two days.

I had the knife in my hand slicing the turkey, and one of the children said something to Vince. He just gave whoever it was a funny look like he didn't want to hear it, and I snapped. I had had enough. I took the knife, pointed it between his eyes, and screamed right in his face, "You lost!" I paused for a second and said it again — "You lost" — and then spelled it slowly and loudly: "L O S T — lost. Do you understand?"

He looked at me with his steel blue eyes just as cold as he could make them and without any change of expression he said, "No shit."

When he said that, we all started laughing, including him, and his awful mood finally left him. We ended up having a great Christmas afternoon. I don't know if all coaches are as intense as Vince, but I know most coaches' wives aren't. We had to learn how to let go and get on with living.

"NO NEW SEX!"

I remember clearly the night we played Vanderbilt in Nashville in 1987. It was in October, and we had won four games and lost two as we headed into that battleground. I had only recently started traveling with Vince, so I was looking forward to the game. Traveling with the team was interesting because it's all business and you get a new perspective on what really goes into a football game. The players read and listened to their headphones. The coaches talked in soft tones or whispers, and I was on my very best behavior. I didn't want to do or say anything that would upset the head coach or anyone else. No one would ever be able to blame a loss on me.

I saw no signs that Vince might not be feeling well. When you live with someone for so long, I don't think you pick up on little things as quickly as you might have a few years earlier. At any rate, I never noticed. All seemed fine to me. He was nervous about his team, but every game was stressful. Never in my wildest imagination did I think anything was wrong with him.

As he later related the story to me, Vanderbilt jumped ahead, 21-7, and after they scored the third touchdown, he began having chest pains down the sternum. He said he put his hand on his chest, looked up at the scoreboard, and began laughing to himself. "This would be a hell of a way to die," he was thinking, "getting beat by Vanderbilt and dropping dead on the sidelines." Sometimes you have to laugh in a crisis, or you will cry.

He said that after we scored and went ahead, his pains went away and he really didn't think anymore about it.

After the game, which we won 52-24, we all boarded the plane and received our sack dinners for the flight home. These are not ordinary sandwiches. They are huge. And there are two of them—usually one turkey and one ham. Both have at least a half-pound of meat and another half-pound of cheese. Accompanying the two sandwiches are a bag of chips, a giant candy bar, and an apple. By the time that we all got on the plane, it was close to midnight, and I knew it was too late for me to eat all that food. I pulled out the apple and watched Vince inhale the turkey sandwich.

The whole time he was eating it, I was nagging him. I kept telling him it was too late to put that much meat in his body and that he ought to eat just the bread and the apple. He finally told me to be quiet; he hadn't eaten since the pregame meal at four and he was hungry! When he gave me his "I've had enough of your nagging" tone of voice, I knew the conversation was over.

I'm not sure he slept at all that night, he had indigestion so bad. Of course, I had no sympathy for him since I had warned him, but he must have consumed a bottle of Mylanta trying to get some relief. I never said a word; I figured he had learned his lesson.

Sunday mornings after football games, Vince had to get up at five in order to get to the TV station to do his weekly show. After a night game he rarely got over an hour or two of sleep. On this morning, he did his show and stopped on the way home and picked up biscuits for breakfast. I love big, thick, hot biscuits, and when he brought them home after his show, it was my treat of the week. He was feeling better and ate a biscuit with me. Later he recalled that it didn't sit well with him.

I left town that afternoon to fly to Houston where I was speaking the next day. Vince went to the office as usual and then went to a special lunch for the inauguration of our new president, Dr. Charles Knapp. He felt fine at lunch, but walking from the Continuing Education Center to the ceremony on Old Campus, he had to walk up a steep hill and got short of breath. He thought to himself, "I can't be this out of shape," but again blamed it on his lack of sleep. Here's a man who works out every day of his life, and he manages to ignore the fact that he had trouble walking up a hill. Sometimes I wonder about his "walking around sense."

I had left him a frozen dinner with complete cooking instructions before I left. He doesn't know how to do oven dinners, but he has learned to work the microwave. After the inauguration and more office work, he came home around eight o'clock to do his exercises, which consisted of a little floor work and then a thirty-minute swim in our pool. He did his floor work and then got in the pool. After about ten minutes of swimming, he got indigestion so bad he had to quit. Of course, it made him furious that he had to stop, so he sat in one of the pool chairs until his indigestion calmed down and then got back in the pool, disgusted that he was unable to complete his workout all at one time. As soon as he was back in the water, his indigestion flared up again. Thank God he had sense enough to stop and wait until the morning to finish his swim. He had his dinner and went to bed early.

The next morning he got up early and began his usual workout, but after ten minutes in the pool he had another violent attack of burping, indigestion pain, and tightness in his chest. Fortunately, he stopped again and decided he would call the doctor when he got to work. Surely those sandwiches weren't still working on him. After a shower, however, he felt fine and got so wrapped up in his work that he forgot about the doctor. Luckily, his secretary, Jean Hunnicutt, made a comment about all of the indigestion tablet wrappers he had discarded the previous day, and that reminded him to call his doctor, Ham Magill.

He went in later that morning, and after he described his weekend experiences, Dr. Magill immediately ordered an angiogram, a dye test that shows any blocked arteries. He told Vince that he needed to schedule it immediately, but Vince said he was flying to Florida that afternoon for an evening speech and he couldn't be away from the team until Thursday evening after their last practice before the Kentucky game on Saturday.

Dr. Magill said, "I think you'd better get someone to make that speech for you tonight in Florida, or you might not be at the game on Saturday."

"You're kidding," said Vince.

"No, I'm not kidding," said Dr. Magill. "I want you in the hospital this afternoon right after practice."

Vince told me later he was still not overly concerned, except for how to find a substitute speaker for his engagement and how to check himself into the hospital with no media attention. As he walked into his office, I was on the phone talking with his secretary. I had just had breakfast in Houston and for some reason felt the urge to talk with Vince, and I knew that this was the usual time for him to be out of his coaching meeting. She told me that she had sent him to the doctor, and I began relating the story about how much he had eaten and how late at night it was and on and on and on, until she broke in and said, "He's walking in the door right now. You can talk to him."

Vince calmly told me that he was having an angiogram and that I was to call the doctor's special number when I landed in Atlanta to find out whether everything was normal, which he was convinced it would be.

I was shaken. I couldn't believe that the doctor thought something might be wrong with Vincent, and here I was in Houston getting ready to make a speech. I wanted to run home, but I knew that I had to calm down. There was nothing I could do but pray, and I began immediately. I promised the Lord everything!

I landed in Atlanta and went to the first pay phone and made the call. I'll never forget Dr. Magill's words.

"Barbara, he's on his way to Emory by ambulance and should be there about the time you arrive. He has blockage in two arteries, and they're going to do an angioplasty on him."

He knew I was in shock and tried to calm me down by telling me how many of these are done every day and how successful they are. But this was my husband, and statistics were irrelevant. My world had started flipping around in a matter of seconds, and I didn't like it. I could not entertain the idea that something so serious was wrong with Vincent. He was the strong one in the family; he wasn't supposed to get sick. That was not in the script.

I'm not sure how I got to Emory Hospital, but I was there in what seemed like seconds. I walked in and saw our three married children and their spouses, my sisters-in-law, who were both in town for shopping, and my sister. And there was Vince, white as a ghost, asking for food with a sheepish grin on his face. So typical—even then he didn't want to miss a meal!

The hospital was keeping Vince's room number a secret in order to keep reporters from hounding him, but as I was leaving that night, I saw one reporter I knew camped out on the floor waiting to find where Vince was. I lost it. I told him in no uncertain terms what I thought about him, his integrity, his paper, and his sneaking around the hospital looking for a story. Couldn't they for once just leave us alone?

But it was big news for the state. "Vince Dooley in hospital with heart problems." "Vince Dooley having angioplasty." Not many people had ever heard of an angioplasty until this happened, and now everyone wanted to know what it was, how the procedure worked, and the prognosis. For three days in Atlanta it was a major story. TV shows were interrupted to show Vince's arteries. They would show his clogged artery, and then they would show how the procedure had unclogged the artery. They had diagrams and pictures of the heart all over the screen. It was the hot topic of conversation that week.

The procedure took place on Tuesday, and he was leaving the hospital on Thursday. The doctors said, without a moment's hesitation, that he could be back on the football field for the game on Saturday. I thought that was a little much, but who am I to argue with a coach and a doctor? Very few do's and don't's were prescribed for his recovery, but there was one I thought was pretty funny.

"Coach," this one doctor said, "I'm a little embarrassed to mention this, but as a doctor I have to cover every situation. Your diet is important, exercise is important, and getting away from stress is important, but another important thing is there can be no new sex."

I almost fell out laughing and just had to ask, "What do you mean?"

He turned red with embarrassment, and I knew he hated my confronting him with more questions. I began teasing Vince about how the Lord had taken care of any middle-age-crazy notions, if there should ever happen to be any. He would forever be sentenced to "old sex."

We left the hospital amid the fanfare of newspaper reporters, television cameras, and every onlooker in the area. It was a circus. Vince held a press conference and assured everyone that he was perfectly fine. On the way out of the hospital, with cameras in our faces, we had an argument.

"Give me the keys," he said.

"No, you are not driving," I informed him.

He said, "I said, give me the keys."

"Are you crazy?" I said. "You just got out of the hospital, and you're a terrible driver even when conditions are perfect. You are not driving."

He gave me a look that I knew not to question, a look that means I've pushed him too far, so I threw him the keys. We got in and drove about two blocks away from the reporters and the cameras, and he pulled over and told me to drive. He didn't want anyone to think that he wasn't in control. That's Vince Dooley: he always has everything under control, and if he doesn't, you aren't supposed to know about it.

It's my opinion that one of the major differences between men and women is in the area of sickness. Women seem to accept being sick much more easily, and they don't dwell on the issue. Men are different. Anything that goes wrong with their bodies, they want to talk about it and talk about it and talk about it. A great clue that middle age has arrived is when you overhear brothers talking about their bowel movements. I'm not sure that I had ever thought about these differences until this little heart problem, but the minute we got on the road to Athens, he began rehashing the whole experience — the initial pains, the angiogram, the ambulance ride to Emory all hooked up to that machine, rolling down the hospital halls on a stretcher. He told how one man had said, "Is that Coach Dooley?" and he immediately grabbed the sheet and pulled it over his face to keep people from recognizing him.

"Do you think a sheet would keep anyone from recognizing you?" I had to interject. "They would recognize that nose under any cover."

Without giving my remark the least notice, he went on talking about being in intensive care and how he loved the attention he got. He didn't like getting moved to the floor, he said, because the nurses weren't always there like they were in intensive care. I threw in, "You get what you pay for," but he kept right on, once again describing the procedure. He talked about how great it was because you are wide awake and can watch everything on a TV monitor. He said it was like watching a film in a coaching meeting, and at one point he even asked, "Doc, can you run that back one more time?" He talked the whole way home, which was unusual, and I listened, which was even more unusual.

We got home, and he went straight to practice. He was determined that he was going to stay with his normal routine. He would go to the office on Friday, talk to the team and let them know that he was okay, and get ready to play Kentucky on Saturday. Meanwhile, whenever anybody would call or come by, he would start from the first pain and go through the complete procedure. He even brought his used "balloons" home so he could show people how they opened his arteries.

Saturday arrived, and he didn't break his schedule. I went to the game not only nervous about who would win but about how Vince would hold up. I didn't think he should be on the sidelines, and I had told both him and the doctor that. But Vince thought it was safer than sitting next to me. The doctor's only advice was, "Don't get too carried away." Let's face it — if you're a competitor, you are either in the game or out; there's no almost.

Vince tried to be "almost" during the first half. He tried not to get into the game and tried to keep calm, and that's the way his team was playing. It looked like they were half asleep out there, and they fell behind. After halftime Vince Dooley got on the sidelines, got into the game, and forgot about his condition. He was a competitor, he wanted to win this game, and to hell with his heart!

We were hoping for a non-stressful game, but as happened in so many of his games, we were behind most of the way and finally pulled it out with a desperate last drive, scoring with less than a minute to play to win. Just the type of game his heart needed.

After games in Athens we always entertain at our home, and this game was no exception. Vince wanted everything to appear normal. He didn't want anyone to think of him as sick. He seemed perfectly fine until everyone left and it was time for bed. He was exhausted, and I thought that he would have no trouble falling asleep. Oh, how wrong I was. He began having chest pains, caused by a combination of indigestion and being "shell-shocked," and was sure that something was wrong.

For the first time in years, I panicked. I didn't want him to drop dead in my den in front of me. I wanted a doctor and a hospital. But he would have no part of that. He said that he had to do his TV show Sunday morning before he would call the doctor. I began to argue, and he promptly told me that my mouth was more stressful than anything else, "so just be quiet and leave me be." I sat quietly on the sofa all night and watched him try to doze. I know that I never closed my eyes, and I don't think he slept either, but he did sit as still as death with his hands crossed over his heart and his eyes closed for the entire night. At five in the morning he showered, went to the TV station, and did his show.

The minute Vincent got back home, we called Dr. Magill and told him about our night. He didn't want to take any chances and decided that to be safe he would do another angiogram. We didn't dread the procedure nearly as much as we dreaded the press. Of course, they would find out about it, and we would be besieged with phone calls and more print. I took him to the hospital, checked him in, and left to go to church. When I came back, the test had been completed and showed all was well, but he had to stay flat on his back for six hours. Knowing that his arteries were open and that he was not going to die that day, he got me to call his coaches so that he could have his meetings in his hospital room to get ready for the next opponent. He's never been one to waste a minute, and he wasn't going to start now.

I picked him up that afternoon about six and brought him home, with strict instructions that he was to do nothing at all but go to bed. He was warned that if he were to start bleeding where the needle had been inserted for the test it could be dangerous. The nurse told him that if it should start bleeding to put his finger on the spot and exert just enough pressure to stop it.

We headed for home, and, of course, the minute we walked into the house, the phone began ringing. The press wanted to know if the rumor that Vince was back in the hospital were true. Vince took the calls as I laid him on the couch with his feet propped up, pillows under his head, the TV going, and a fire in the fireplace. What more could a man want? I went to the kitchen to start fixing dinner. I was starving. In the meantime, Hamp McWhorter came to visit and to see if there was anything he could do for us. When Derek left for Virginia, Hamp practically became our adopted son and was always coming by to check on us. He sat down in the kitchen with me, and I fixed him a plate of food. I hate to eat alone, and Vince had already informed me that he was not hungry. That was an historical first!

Vince was out of our line of sight, on the phone trying to assure a reporter that all was fine. Hamp and I were in the kitchen eating and talking when we saw a magazine go sailing across the den. Vince was still talking on the phone but had thrown a magazine!

"Hamp, I think he's lost it," I said. "Did you see that magazine go sailing across the room or was that my imagination?"

Vince was still talking on the phone, and all of a sudden we saw his shoe go sailing across the room and slam into the wall. Hamp jumped up and ran in the den to see what was going on. I kept on eating. I had had enough for one day. Vince hung up the phone, and I heard him say, "Just lay me on the floor carefully." Without getting up, I screamed, "What's going on, Hamp?"

"I think Coach Dooley is about to faint," he said. "He's bleeding."

I jumped up, ran to the den, and said, "Slide him on the floor because I don't want blood on the carpet." Can you believe that thought came into my mind? I looked down, and Vince had no color in his face. He had a small drop of blood on his undershorts, which had prompted him to put so much pressure on his leg with his thumb that it cut off all of his circulation. He never has been able to do anything halfway. Instead of mild pressure, he squeezed the poor artery completely shut, and between that and his inability to tolerate a little blood, especially his own, he was totally out of it. Mr. Coach had been brought to the floor by a drop of his own blood.

What a nightmare the whole week had been, but a lot of laughs once we knew that everything was alright. Wherever we went, whatever the conversation, we always ended up talking about his heart. He was obsessed with it. He read everything he could read and talked with anybody who had ever had any heart problems. We would go to parties, and before the night was over you would see a group of men in a circle around Vince, and you could bet they were talking about the heart. The ones who had had open-heart surgery were not above opening their shirts and comparing scars.

It amazed me. When women have serious operations, they are expected to come home and get back into their regular routines without a mention of how they feel. They usually walk into a mess and within hours after surgery are trying, however feebly, to pick up or wash a dish. Not so with the stronger sex. They talk about it for days or months and want to compare notes with anyone who has had something similar. Can you imagine a group of women standing around at a party comparing scars? Most don't want to admit that they have a scar.

One morning I called my mother to visit and was telling her how tired I was of listening to Vince talk about his angioplasty. I said, "Mother, he's driving me crazy. That's all he wants to talk about, and I've heard the story so many times that I could give you a blow-by-blow and not miss a line. I'm sick of it."

She very calmly and wisely said, "I'm sure there are a lot of young ladies who would love for him to tell them his story." I immediately ran into the den and said, "Vince, tell me about your heart again!"

I was patient for as long as I could be, and when I knew that he was healthy both physically and mentally again, I took off the kid gloves and began treating him with my old spunk. One night after dinner he began his heart story, and I knew I couldn't listen again.

"Honey," I said, "I've seen President Johnson's scar on TV, I've seen President Reagan's prostate on TV, I've seen Mrs. Reagan's boob on TV, and I've seen your arteries on TV. I just praise God that you didn't have hemorrhoids or your ass would have been on TV."

He looked up and said, "I don't think you understand. My ass is on TV every Saturday."

A few years after his heart problem, Vince discovered that he had a hernia. He had been watching this place in his groin area for almost two years and had been to several doctors, but they all explained that the swelling was a natural result of Vince's having been "cathed" so many times for angiograms. He would not give up. He went from doctor to doctor until he finally found a surgeon who took one look at him and said he had a hernia and needed to have an operation. This was a shock to his system. That there was something else wrong with his strong, athletic body was a thought that he didn't like to entertain.

When he came back from the doctor and explained his hernia to me, he said, "Periodically my intestines are going to come out, and I'll have to lie down and twist them back in."

Well, I couldn't take much of that, so I told him right up front that I didn't want to hear any talk about his hernia or his intestines, and I certainly had no intention of watching him twist his intestines back in place.

Finally, he made the decision to go in and have it operated on. For some reason, and I don't know what it is, doctors never seem to spell out exactly how bad an operation is going to be. All Vince heard from every doctor he talked to was, "No problem; this is a piece of cake. In fact, we do this as out-patient work now. You probably need to spend one night, but not any more than that, and you should be at work in three or four days without any problem at all."

I listened to him tell me how easy this operation was going to be, and I didn't say anything because I could've been wrong, but I know this: when I've been cut, it's not that easy. But all went well. He stayed overnight in the hospital and came home on a Saturday afternoon, at which time we put him on the couch, turned on the TV, and began to wait on him hand and foot. The doctor's instructions were simple: "He can do what he feels like doing, but be sure he takes his pain pills with him. And,

Barbara, do not let him lift anything for the next six weeks."

Well, I looked at the doctor with a shocked expression and said, "Doc, that certainly won't be a problem. He hasn't lifted anything in thirty-two years. I'm certainly not going to worry about him in the next six weeks."

Forty-eight hours after his surgery, which was Sunday morning, he got up and got dressed and decided he would go to church with us. Of course, I could have told him not to, but I didn't. All of the children were home, and he wanted to show them that he was not a wimp. The doctor had told him to do what he wanted to do, and that's exactly what he was going to do. He went to church, but by the end of Mass it was obvious he needed to get home and back to bed.

We got him home and put him on the couch, and he didn't move the rest of the day. At five-thirty Monday morning, I woke to the sound of the shower running in the bathroom and lights on in the closet. I was determined not to get angry, but I was so mad at him for disturbing my sleep that I laid in the bed with the covers over my head and prayed that I would have the peace and calm that I needed. There's nothing worse than to get mad first thing in the morning and start the day off wrong. Plus, I had to remember that he was sick and I had to pamper him.

Out of the corner of my eye I watched him slowly but methodically get dressed. Not only was he determined to go to work, but, because of his pride, he was going to work long before anybody else so that no one could see that he couldn't walk very well. And I was going to drive him. I took him to work and opened the door of his office for him at 6:45. He wanted to put in a good half-day, and I was instructed to come back at twelve-thirty to pick him up. I objected to the whole idea, but I knew from experience that there was no point in my saying anything. His mind was made up.

When I arrived to pick him up, he was in severe pain. He couldn't even stand up straight. Not only was he in severe pain, but, as I later discovered, his testicles and his whole groin area had swollen about three times their normal size.

I got him on the couch and put an ice bag on the affected area to reduce the swelling. As I got him all situated, my mind began playing games with me. I remembered all the times I had had babies or serious operations and how the only thing that was ever on Vince's mind was how soon I could have sex. You can talk to women in all walks of life, and they will tell you the same story. The minute you have a baby, the first thing your husband will say is, "Only six more weeks."

There you are, sore, swollen, and exhausted. Sex is the last thing on your mind. You don't even want to think about it, but he's ready. It's a situation we all face and bravely try to smile about. Well, I thought this was an appropriate time to go after him. It was payback time! There he was on the couch, swollen, in pain, just wanting to be left alone. I put my arm around him and said, "Honey, how about a little sex?"

He looked at me totally without humor, totally without love, with only horror on his face, and said, "You are totally deranged. If the sight of this arouses you, you are sick and have a serious problem."

I started laughing and thought with satisfaction how everything that goes around comes around.

THE LAST FLEDGLING

Derek wanted to go to a Division 1-A school because he felt like he could play football at the highest college level, and as he told me later, he didn't want to wake up when he was forty years old and wish he had done it. I had to respect that, so we decided to go look at college campuses.

One of the first schools that came to Derek's mind was the University of Virginia. It was a great academic school, Division 1-A, and he felt like he would have a chance to play if he could go there. So we took a visit to Virginia, and immediately he fell in love with it. Derek is a very smart young man and has used his talents to the best of his ability. He was class president in high school and also valedictorian, so he had a very good grade point average. And we felt that with a high SAT he could get into the University of Virginia. In the meantime, he had taken trips to both Princeton and Yale, but they paled in comparison to Virginia.

One of the most interesting incidents I remember from Derek's decision-making period was the afternoon the head coach from Princeton came by to recruit him. Coach Ron Rogerson (who has since passed away) came to see us and sat in our back den and began telling us why Derek should come to Princeton. I got the biggest kick out of that because for twenty-three years I had been listening to Vince recruit, helping Vince recruit, and here we were on the other end. It was a wonderful experience to feel so important and so wanted, and I remember thinking that Derek probably ought to go to Princeton; they wanted him so badly. But after Derek went up there and visited, he said he just didn't feel quite at home.

While he was at Princeton on his weekend visit, he went to a party the students were having, and Brooke Shields happened to be there. He said he didn't want to turn and look and yet he did want to turn and look. She was standing right behind him for about fifteen minutes, and finally when he got the nerve to turn around and look at her, she was leaving. His big chance to meet Brooke was gone.

While he was at the same party, some young lady at Princeton came up to talk to him and found out that he was from the great state of Georgia. She immediately went into a rant against the South, talking about slavery and landowners and sharecroppers, and Derek decided to have a little fun with her: "Uh, well, I understand what you're talking about, but you know we just have a small farm down there. We only have twenty-five slaves on our plantation, and our plantation's only two hundred acres. We certainly don't mistreat anyone. We take care of them, we feed them, we clothe them, we take them to the doctor. We do so much more for our slaves than you do for your friends up North." He could tell that she was getting more and more riled, and he was just loving every minute of it. Finally she looked at him and said, "You Southern Pig!" and turned around and walked off. When he came home and told me the story, I knew that Princeton was out for Derek.

Now the problem was going to be to convince his father that UVA was the school of his choice, and that was going to be a difficult job because Vincent's mind was made up that Derek was going to either Princeton or Yale. Vincent wanted him to go to an Ivy League school for the education and also because the classification was 1-AA (not quite as competitive), and he thought Derek would have a better chance of a rewarding football experience. I knew it was going to be the Battle of the Wills, and I was interested to see how Derek would pull it off. With the other three children, it usually didn't matter what they wanted to do. Vincent seemed always to be able to influence them, but Derek had grown up almost by himself after they had gone and had learned how to deal with his dad. And he and I knew that to deal with his dad he had to be alert and organized; that was the way to win his war.

So every day we talked about why he should go to Virginia. We discussed the advantages of Virginia over Princeton, and it always boiled down to, first, a great education, and second, Division 1-A football. For some reason he was determined that he could walk on, earn a scholarship, and contribute to their program. I was still convinced that he could walk on at Georgia and earn a scholarship, but I would never have wanted him to do that. If his father could not give him a scholarship outright because he did deserve it, then I didn't want his son to play for him. And as I look back on it, I think Vince's hands were tied. His son really wasn't a prospect that every school wanted, and had he signed Derek, he would have been widely accused of favoritism. So rather than put himself and Derek into such a situation, he knew in his heart the right thing to do was for Derek to go away to school. I knew it, too, but I played it for all it was worth. I wanted him to know how much I was going to miss my baby.

Decision day finally arrived, and Vince told Derek that he would be home that evening to discuss it. That afternoon Derek said to me, "Mom, I'm going to Virginia. What am I going to do to convince him?" We set up our game plan. I told him that the best way to influence his dad was to go upstairs and literally to write down, point by point, the reasons for going and the reasons for not going. Then when his dad came home to talk to him, he would have it all laid out in an organized fashion. But I knew it was going to be a tough evening.

After dinner the two went into the den, and I knew to stay away because I certainly didn't want my mouth to interfere like it normally did. And the only way for me to stay out of the conversation was just to remove myself from the area. So I was doing the dishes and trying to eavesdrop, and I heard Derek going point by point over why he should go to the University of Virginia. I think he talked about thirty minutes non-stop, making his points and backing them up. When he finally finished, his father had not said a word; he had just sat there and listened and looked. Really there was nothing Vince could say. He knew in his heart he had been defeated. He stood up, put his hand out, and shook Derek's hand and said, "Well, congratulations, son. You've made a wise decision."

We were all very excited over Derek's choice, but I knew eight hours was a long way from home and I would not get to see my baby nearly as often as I had wanted to. I also knew that it was going to be very difficult for me, as the head coach's wife, to ever get to see Derek play because I had so many responsibilities at home during football season. I was torn as to whether to go to see Derek play or to stay here and assume my duties as Vince's wife, but Vince and I talked it over and worked out a compromise. I would go to all of Virginia's home games that did not fall on a Georgia home game. That seemed satisfactory, at least for the time being, and it turned out that by the time Derek was a regular—his last two years—I was able to get to most of his home games.

But the thought of Derek Dooley leaving for school was just about more than I could take. For a week before he left, as we were packing and getting his things ready, I was choking up. Whenever he would talk about it, I would start to lose it. So the day before he left, he came in and said, "Now Mom, I can't go through this crying thing with you." He said, "I'm writing out a contract right now, and you're going to sign it. It says if you cry when you leave me at school, you're going to have to pay me a hundred dollars."

Well, Derek knows how tight I am when it comes to giving the children money. Vincent and I have always felt that giving the children too much money could cause serious problems, and we've always made them work for their spending money. So when Derek wrote that contract, he knew that was a lot of money for me to be handing over to him. What he didn't know was how much being able to cry would be worth to me. That afternoon after I signed his contract, I went to the bank and I got me a hundred-dollar bill. I had a funny feeling that this was one contract I was going to break.

The next day we got up early, and Vincent and I drove Derek to Virginia. It was a gorgeous drive, and all the way up we had a wonderful time, but I had this hollow feeling in the pit of my stomach knowing that my son was getting ready to leave. Honestly, I was about to die.

Finally, we got there and found out where he was supposed to be and saw all the other parents unloading their children. Derek didn't want us to even hang around. We unloaded the car, and he walked over and said, "Well, Mom, I guess this is it" and bent down to kiss me. Needless to say, I broke down and sobbed. Derek said, "Mom, remember the contract." I reached into my pocket and pulled out the hundred-dollar bill and said, "Here, I can cry all I want to." With that I went into a shoulder-shaking crying jag, and I don't think I stopped crying the whole eight hours back to Athens. I'm not sure that Vincent ever said a word to me. I just cried the whole eight hours.

When we got home and walked in the door, it felt like the emptiest house in the world. I can't even explain the feeling. Now we had nobody here. It was just the two of us, and I really wasn't sure that we would have anything to say — or if we really liked each other. This was really going to be a test of our marriage.

I was tired, I was drained from crying, and I went straight to bed. When I'm depressed I can always go to bed and feel a little bit better when I wake up. The sun always does rise after a good night's sleep, but the next morning it was really quiet. There was nobody to get breakfast for except Vincent, and he had a cup of coffee, a bowl of cereal, and a newspaper. There was nobody to visit with, no noise, no school. It was just two adults in a big empty house.

Vince and I tried to make small talk at breakfast, but not much. I was not in the mood and he knew it, so he left for work thinking he would give me a day to get myself organized. That day I can remember going up to Derek's room and throwing myself across his bed and sobbing just as if he had died. I could not have been more miserable, I don't think. He was gone, my heart and soul, my baby; the last one was now gone. This was the start of a new period in my life, and as I look back on it, I think I was crying not only because Derek was gone but also because I wasn't ready to face my new life.

But while I cried, I realized that I had to get myself together. This was the craziest thing in the whole wide world. I had left a perfectly healthy, wonderful, intelligent, human being at Charlottesville, Virginia, and here I was acting like a baby. So I picked myself up that day, got dressed, and went about my errands trying to think only positive thoughts. No negatives — that was my deal for the day. And I decided that that night I was going to have a romantic dinner. It was probably the first night in our married life that we were together in that house all by ourselves. It was a strange feeling — but what a wonderful opportunity! So I set the table for two (a weird experience in itself), got out candles, and used my best china and silver. When Vince came home, I had a special meal for him and a bottle of wine.

I knew it was just the two of us now, and I knew we had to decide that we really liked each other, so I was going the whole nine yards. I served dinner, Vincent said the blessing, and the next thing I knew he had the newspaper in front of him. I couldn't believe it. All of a sudden, with the first bite of food in my mouth, tears started streaming down my face. Slowly the newspaper came down, and Vince said, "Barbara, what is wrong with you?"

"I just miss Derek so much I can't stand it," I said.

"What do you mean?" he said. "Here we are, just the two of us, having a nice, quiet, romantic evening, and you're missing Derek. How do you think that makes me feel?''

"At least Derek talks," I answered. "All you do is read the paper."

Well, I think it dawned on him right then that he was going to have to baby-sit me. He was going to have to learn to talk to me because there was nobody else in this house to pay attention to me but him. And I have to say that he has taken on the job well. We have learned to talk, and he doesn't read the paper anymore at the table. He's it, and we both know the importance of communication.

When people tell us what great kids we have, we're proud; we're proud of the fact that they have developed into such good citizens and such good people. All four of them are very good people. When I look back and wonder why they did turn so out well, I don't know—I think it's luck. But I also think a lot of it is communication. Our children knew every single day not only that we loved them, but also how we felt about things, about everything. I believe they knew where we stood on every topic ever brought up in our home. I think it's sad when you ask a child how his mother or father feels about something, and the child replies, "Oh, she doesn't care," or "He doesn't care," or "It doesn't make any difference to them." That wasn't the way it was around the Dooley household.

I have never really understood the empty-nest syndrome, and if I did in fact have it, it didn't last very long. In fact, when I look back now on my life, I don't know when I really had time to work the children in. When Derek left and I got used to the idea, I can honestly say that Vince and I began having real fun together for the first time since we had our first child. I felt that the responsibility of the children was off my shoulders for the first time in twenty years or so. I no longer had to worry about somebody being at home when we weren't there. Now we were free, and it was an exuberant freedom. It meant, for instance, that if we were in Atlanta and didn't feel like driving home we could just pull over and check into a hotel. We didn't have to call anybody; we didn't have to worry that somebody might be having a party or getting in trouble while we were gone. It was a liberating feeling that I had never experienced before, and now as I reflect back on our lives I'm not so sure that it isn't the greatest feeling I've ever had.

We were so young when we had children that we never really had time to get to know each other as a couple. I think that's what caused a lot of our problems when I was in my thirties; we never really had a solid friendship, a deep knowledge of each other, before the children came, and once children come into your life they take so much out of it. They are every day, all day until they leave for college and marry, and then you might have a little bit of relief from thinking about them.

One of the neatest things that we experienced was the opportunity to carry on a conversation without any interruptions. It was amazing. When Vince would start a sentence, it didn't matter how long it took him to finish it; nobody was there interrupting. But I must say that sometimes it takes Vince a long time to finish a sentence. I've known him to start a sentence at breakfast and finish it after he's gone back to his room, brushed his teeth, put on his coat and tie, and is walking out the door to go to work. His thought processes sometimes take a long time, and usually there was somebody else here to jump in and take up the slack. But with just the two of us, I really noticed how long it took him to finish a thought. One day I asked him why he couldn't just deliver one whole sentence right off of the top of his head without stopping. He said it was because when he begins one sentence about five other thoughts crowd into his brain, and he just never thinks about ending the sentence he started. It's a remarkable process.

In 1987, a most interesting scenario was shaping up. The University of Georgia opened up its football season with the University of Virginia. This was Derek's second year, he had made the traveling squad, and he was excited about Virginia coming to Athens — between the hedges. He told all of his teammates about how awesome it was and how tough Georgia was but how he knew Virginia could beat them. I must have talked to him every day for a couple of weeks, and he was telling me how they were coming here to beat us between the hedges.

Meanwhile, I was moaning to Vince, "Who am I going to pull for?" I had my son coming here, and yet I was going to be sitting in Georgia's press box wearing red and black with my husband the head coach, so what was I going to do? Was I going to yell for my husband or was I going to yell for my son? I thought maybe I ought to yell for my son to do the very best he could do but yell for Georgia to win. Now, how do you do that? I didn't know, but I thought about it and I thought about it, and I talked to Vince about it. "What should I do?" I asked. "I've gotta pull for Derek. I know you'll understand."

Finally one morning he said to me, "Barbara, you've got to calm down and think about what you're saying. You've got to realize who butters your bread."

I thought about it a minute and realized, yeah, Vince is right, and then I said, "You better think about who you sleep with."

Derek didn't get to play very much that day, but I was delighted just to go to the visiting team's locker room and watch him walk out. What a proud moment I felt.

November 17, 1990, came just as scheduled, and I had planned to be there. It was Derek's last home football game, and the Virginia Athletic Department was honoring all the seniors' parents at halftime. I mentioned going to Vincent, and he informed me that Georgia would be playing Auburn that day and he had a commitment to his job to be at Auburn. I didn't argue or even persist. I said no more and made my plans to go. I really never thought any more about it. He has always put his job first, and I was used to it — or so I thought.

I don't know of one head coach's wife in the country who hasn't been both father and mother to her children. They have all picked up the slack that a head football coach's life creates, and most of them don't complain until we all get together. When we meet at coaches' clinics throughout the year, we compare lives and always feel better knowing that we aren't the only one going through life pulling a full load. The interesting thing about our lives is that our children have been trained, quite subconsciously, not to expect their dads to do anything or be anywhere, but they expect their mothers to be at every event and take part in every activity they are involved in. And, of course, we do, and we love doing it, but sometimes we long for our other half to share it with.

Saturday was no exception. Derek wanted me there at his final home game to be presented at halftime with the other parents. He didn't expect his father to come, nor did I think about it until halftime started and all of the parents walked on the field arm in arm. They began calling names,

"Mr. and Mrs. − −, parents of − −," "Mr. & Mrs. − −, parents of − −." And then I heard, "Barbara Dooley, mother of Derek Dooley." I was the only parent on the field by myself. (I can feel sorry for myself.) My emotions took over at once, and tears began streaming down my face as I accepted his jersey as my gift from the UVA Athletic Department.

It was a glorious fall afternoon with bright sunshine and a deep blue sky. The stands were full of students and alumni clapping and cheering for the young men who had helped bring Virginia to new football heights. I was crying, thinking how fast the past five years had gone . . . the goals that Derek had set and had achieved . . . how proud I was of him. I felt sorry for Vince that he once again had put his job first and had missed yet another milestone in one of his children's lives. And then my sympathy for him turned to anger—why even at this stage of our lives did his job have to come first?

I stood on the field and looked all around me, knowing that another chapter of my life was closing. Our baby was finishing his football career, finishing his college career, and entering the adult world, and I was having to face it all alone. Vincent has always preached to us that nothing worthwhile in life is free, and you have to be willing to pay the price for any achievement. He has paid an enormous price for his success.

"RUN, VINCENT, RUN!"

I'm not sure when the word politics entered our relationship, but I am sure that it caused a lot of commotion when it did. For so many years I never really thought about Vincent being anything but a head football coach. I never even thought about him being just athletic director. That seemed a sobering kind of job, if not downright boring. Never could he be happy out of coaching. Oh, how wrong I was!

History had always been a love of his, and wars and politics intrigued him. He read every chance he got, and he loved to be in an academic atmosphere and just talk history. He would always tell me that everything in life repeated itself and that if you read history you could understand what was happening in our world today. I never thought that I would live long enough to see history repeat itself, so I was never really that interested in reading his books, though I loved listening to him talk about how current events related to events in the past. He would even relate football seasons and teams to different periods of history, and he sometimes drew parallels between his handling of some coaching crisis and the way political leaders of the past had handled their crises. Drawing analogies from politics was one thing, but entering politics was another.

Nevertheless, in the spring of 1985, some politician called Vince and asked if he had ever thought about running for office. Republican Matt Mattingly was in the U.S. Senate, and the Democrats wanted that seat back. Mattingly had upset Talmadge, and the Democrats weren't too happy about it. They wanted a candidate with name recognition, an intelligent candidate, and a candidate who could beat Mattingly. They decided Vince was that candidate.

At first Vince didn't take it too seriously, but the more he thought about it and the more people he talked to, the more that he liked the idea. He had done just about all he could do in the coaching profession, and this seemed like a great new beginning. We both felt that we had been very fortunate in everything life had dealt us and that running for public office would be a great way to give back to the community. Ethyl Kennedy once stated that politics "is the highest form of service," and we both believe that. Vince quietly went about exploring the possibility of getting into the race, and we were getting excited about this new challenge.

The key was that it had to be kept quiet until after football season because he couldn't let his political ambitions affect his football team. Unfortunately, the press got wind of the story the day we were leaving for Europe for our vacation, and by the time that we arrived at the Atlanta airport, every camera and every microphone in the city was waiting for us. Vince admitted that he was thinking about it, but would make no decision until we got back from our trip.

Ironically and quite coincidentally, Senator Talmadge and his wife, Linda, were on our trip, so for the next two weeks Vince had someone to really talk with about his future. Most of the professional politicians whom Vincent had talked to before our trip had advised him to quit coaching immediately in order to start raising money for the campaign. They knew that Mattingly had a war chest ready for the fight, and the Democrat who challenged him had to have money. But Senator Talmadge told Vince that he didn't have to do a thing until the first of the year. He said that Vince had enough name recognition to be able to catch up with no problem. I will admit it was an exciting possibility, but it was also frightening. In fact, my stomach went queasy when I thought about going from the certain to the uncertain, but I was willing to do whatever he wanted to do.

One of the funniest stories that I remember about that two weeks of turmoil was one afternoon when we were having tea with Senator Talmadge and Linda somewhere in the Norwegian Fjords. I have to admit that I love clothes, I love makeup, I love jewelry, I love perfume, and I just love being a girl. I guess I always have. Mother said that even in my tomboy days I still wanted jewelry and perfume. Senator Talmadge looked at me across the table and said, "Barbara, if you are serious about this politics business, then you've got to do some changing."

"What do you mean?" I asked. "Surely I won't have to be quiet, will I?"

In that heavy Southern drawl like nobody else's, he said, "Barbara, you've got to take off your jewelry, wash that makeup off your face, get you a K-Mart dress, and learn how to sweat.''

Even though the media hounded us from the minute we landed back in Atlanta, Vince stuck to his timetable and made his decision a week after he returned from Europe. He decided to ''pass,'' which was certainly inconsistent with his ''run'' philosophy in football. His reasoning, however, was sound. It was two weeks before the players reported for fall practice, and he felt that he could not disrupt the football program that he had worked so hard to build. The president told him that he would have to resign immediately if he had any intentions of running for the senate, which was the way he also felt. He could not in clear conscience leave his team and his coaches in that kind of confusion right before the season. So he put that ambition to rest.

The next political race that might interest him would be the governor's race of 1990, but he would just wait and see what the future would hold.

Once he got a mind-set to get into politics, it never really left him. We talked about it periodically, but never really seriously until 1988. That year would be his twenty-fifth coaching anniversary and an appropriate number to retire on. During the summer we talked it over with our son-in-law, Lindsey, a lawyer who loves politics, and our good friends Nick and Patti, as well as all of our children. Only the family knew that he was thinking about the possibility of quitting after the season.

It was a hard burden for me to carry because I looked at every game as final. I saw everything that season as possibly the ''last one.'' Vince worked just as hard as he did his first year, but every loss was really difficult because I thought it might well be his last season. I wanted him to win the Southeastern Conference championship so badly that it took me months to recover from the Kentucky loss that year. That game truly prevented our championship. I couldn't understand why God couldn't grant us that one favor. I wasn't asking for a national championship. I just wanted all the SEC games and to beat Tech. Was that really too much? Evidently it was because it was not to be. I became very melancholy about every game and every trip. I absorbed every detail that I had taken for granted through the years because I wanted to make sure that I remembered it all. I think it was like being told that you are dying and you don't really want to let go.

Toward the end of the season, everyone was talking about Vince retiring. I think if he hadn't, he might have disappointed a lot of people because they were all playing the guessing game. And the whole season I was trying to act really cool about the whole thing. No final decision had been made, but I knew he was thinking seriously about it. My response to anyone who asked was always, "Where in the world did you get that from?"

We lost that year to South Carolina, Kentucky, and Auburn, and my guts were hanging out over losing the conference championship. We should have won it that last time. I even thought that maybe not winning the SEC would make Vince decide to continue coaching. The day we played Georgia Tech, I was a wreck. I really didn't want to go to the stadium because I was so afraid that we might lose. I had already made up my mind that he was surely not quitting if Tech beat us. We were not going out like that! I went through all the motions of a normal game day, but I was not mentally with it. I was wringing my hands by nine o'clock that morning, something I usually didn't do till kickoff. Then I left the house and forgot my tickets, a first in twenty-five seasons! I think I really didn't want to be at that game, but I knew I had to take the pain one more time.

But our team played great, and the victory gave Vince his 200th victory. It also gave us an 8-3 season and a bid to the Gator Bowl. This was a great way to end his career, even if we weren't conference champs, because it was in this very bowl that Vincent finished his playing career at Auburn with a blaze of glory. Maybe history does repeat itself.

As soon as he officially announced his retirement from coaching, the media immediately asked him about his political intentions. He could not deny that he was interested in the possibility of running for governor, but he stated that he was not jumping into the political race until he had time to think and evaluate. As in the past, no one gave him that time. Everywhere he went, reporters were swarming. All of the speeches that had been on his calendar for months became political rather than sports oriented. Rotary clubs that normally had fifty people at their meetings had 150 if Vince was the speaker. It was overwhelming.

Vincent was exhausted from the football season, and the media were not letting up. He would not be allowed to have any respite before making a decision. That is the price he paid for his tremendous public visibility. He had swapped one hell for another and at one-fourth the pay!

But I was excited about his running for governor. I felt that our state needed some fresh leadership from someone who owed nothing politically to anyone. He would truly be the "people's governor." He is honest, hardworking, and God-fearing, and what more could the people of Georgia want?

It was obvious that some political candidates were nervous at the possibility of Vince in the race, and we were getting a lot of feedback about what it would be like if we did join the real live politicians. Vince was determined that if he did run, he would have an honest, open race with no under-the-table shenanigans, so he decided to report an incident that had occurred a few years prior to his retirement. I call it the Case of the Mustached Blonde, but others know it as the GBI incident.

It started in January of 1983 when Vince was on a recruiting trip with our line coach, Alex Gibbs. They were staying at the Airport Marriott Hotel, and when Vince checked in, he received a message from Alex, who had arrived earlier, asking him to meet him in the lounge. Vince met him there, and while they were talking about the next day's schedule, two women came over to Vince and asked for his autograph. They told him what great Georgia fans they were. This happens to him all of the time, so I know he didn't think that it was unusual.

The unusual thing to me that Vince didn't pick up on was that they continued talking and sat down, uninvited. Later, when he was recalling the story to me, I jumped right in and told him that should have been his first clue to get out! Usually when women, or men for that matter, ask for an autograph, they don't sit down. But these two joined in like they were old friends, and in the course of the conversation they told Vince that they were GBI agents.

I'm sure he started asking them questions about their job. That's just the way he is; he would never hurt anyone's feelings by being abrupt. But he told me that after a few minutes with them at the table he began feeling uneasy and excused himself and went to his room. Not before one of them asked him to dance, however. When he got to this point in the story, I knew it was going to be a whopper! He tried to tell her that he really didn't dance to fast music, (which I knew was not true), so she insisted on dancing when a slow number was played. Again, not wanting to hurt her feelings (can you believe this Southern gentleman? and I think of all the times he's turned me down for a dance), he got on the dance floor, and he said he immediately knew that she was packing a gun. That certainly will get your attention! At any rate, as soon as the dance was over, he excused himself and went straight to his room.

Later, he was in his room talking on the phone with his brother Billy when he heard a knock on the door. (That's the major clue to his innocence, calling his brother and not me.) He asked Bill to wait as he went to the door. Now, I would never open the door to someone that I didn't know. But he did. He didn't even ask who it was; he just flung open the door. Stupid point number two!

A girl was standing there saying she wanted to talk to him. He stuttered for a second, then told her that he was on the phone and that he would be off in a minute. She walked right into his room as he went back to the phone. Now the plot thickens. Vince got off the phone and asked her what she wanted. She didn't answer; she just looked around the room. He then thought that maybe she was a prostitute and asked her if she was. I immediately chimed in with, "How much did she charge?" but he didn't think that was very cute. Again he got no answer, so he got up to lead her to the door and asked her again what she wanted. This time she made a sniffing-like gesture with her nose. He quickly got her out of the room and, after a sigh of relief, decided that she was involved in some drug deal and had knocked on the wrong door.

Vince went on to bed without thinking too much more about it until he saw Alex the next morning and told him the weird story. Alex concurred with Vince's theory that she had gone to the wrong room looking for drugs. Vince chalked it up as a crazy incident, dismissed it from his mind, and got back on the recruiting trail. Dismissed it, that is, until our good friend Don Leebern called several months later and said, "What is this I hear about a GBI report involving you and drugs?" Vince was shocked and at first didn't know what he was talking about. Don didn't really know a lot about it, but a friend had told him that something had been filed with the GBI. The only thing Vince could think of was the weird incident at the Marriott.

He immediately called our good friend and lawyer, Nick Chilivis, and told him what Don had heard. Nick started laughing. Then Vince related the story about the GBI agents coming to his table that night in Atlanta. Nick called and got the file on Vince, and sure enough there was an actual written report about drugs being offered for sex. Now this was when I went into hysteria. Vince Dooley exchanging drugs for sex. That was a hoot! Here is a man who barely drinks a glass of wine, and I'm not ready to report on his sex life, but let me tell you this, I know he's smart enough not to proposition a GBI officer or even a friend of a GBI officer.

Of course, the report was ludicrous, and Nick told us that the GBI officer who filed it was reprimanded for her actions. Nevertheless, when Vince was seriously thinking about running for governor, he decided that he should tell the media about the incident. He knew that some people, and some politicians, had heard rumors, and that these rumors would surface during a campaign. He wanted to be up front before he made the decision to run. He wanted to tell his story so there could be no behind-the-scenes whispers or innuendos.

I thought it was a great idea until he did it. But the morning I woke up and saw the headlines, I almost died. I knew what a lie it was, and it broke my heart to see the sensationalism it caused. The TV news even ran film of the hotel. I was sick to my stomach all day until I was watching the evening news and saw a picture of the GBI agent. I started laughing uncontrollably. She was either ugly or not very photogenic, and it looked like she had a mustache. I said to Vince, "If you tried to proposition her, you must be hard up!"

After going through that, I really was tired of being such a public family. I wasn't sure that I wanted him in politics. I've never minded defending what I believe, but to have to defend against lies was more than I could take. It's really scary to think that anyone can get you at any time if they really set out to, and I just didn't want to be in that position again. But I knew that Vince still wanted to get involved in our state's politics, and I knew how much he has to offer, so I kept quiet.

As the weeks went by, I could tell that he was getting frazzled. He was used to an organized life, and he now felt that his life was out of control. He was tired and needed some time just to regroup, but the press wouldn't leave him alone. One morning, after a couple of sleepless nights, he looked at me and said, "I'm not going to do it."

"Do what?" I asked. Sometimes he speaks in the middle of a thought, and I'm supposed to know what he's talking about.

"I'm not going to run for governor," he said.

"You're crazy," I told him. "You've got to run, the state needs you, and you'll be the best governor we've ever had."

"No," he said, "I have yet to wake up in the morning a single day this past month and feel good about this. My heart is not in it like it needs to be, and I need to listen to my heart over my head."

I knew that he had made his decision and there was really no use talking about it.

The interesting thing about this whole scenario is that I had prayed daily that Jesus would guide us in this decision. I prayed that He would open and close doors so that, whatever the decision, we would know that it came from Him. And yet, when Vince made the decision, and though I knew in my heart that it was what we were supposed to do, I had an unbelievably hard time accepting it. It's so hard for me to be quiet and listen. Someone later said that it was a good thing that Vince didn't run for governor and win because all the roads in Georgia would have double yellow lines going down the middle for "no passing." Not a bad line, and imagining all those yellow-striped highways reminds me of one of the funniest incidents that happened during this period of Vince's political ambitions. But first I have to back up and tell you a little about my own driving habits.

I have been stopped so many times through the years for speeding that you would think I would learn to watch the speedometer and slow down. To be perfectly honest, I never think to look at the speedometer. I just seem to go with the flow, or maybe I should say, ahead of the flow. This tendency seems to get me in trouble. Another thing I never seem to do is look in my rearview mirror when I am on an interstate. I get so lost in my thoughts or in my conversation that I forget to look behind me. Once I had a patrolman's blue light on me for miles before I actually saw him. When I did pull over, he was furious, and I knew there was no possible way to say anything that would help matters.

Now, Vince is another matter. He is a terrible driver, and if there were a more descriptive word than terrible, it would be applicable also. He finds driving a total waste of time, and while he does not usually speed, he is definitely a mobile hazard. He reads his mail, dictates, talks on the phone, reads the paper, and anything else he can think of, so that he doesn't "waste time" driving. He is a lot more dangerous than I am, though I admit I speed.

One thing is for certain: no matter what he gets stopped for—speeding, passing illegally, running a stop sign—he almost never gets a ticket. I have always thought it was unjust and unfair that I had to pay up, but he would get off. We talked about it often, and finally he said to me one day after a heated discussion over my latest ticket, "Barbara, you are just not humble enough. Of course, they are going to ticket you when you give them a smart-ass look and try to talk your way out of it."

"I cannot believe you think you are humble," I snapped back. "What are you talking about?"

"Well," he began in his typically slow manner, "when you get stopped, the first thing you should do is jump out of the car and say, 'Gosh, Officer, I'm sorry. I didn't realize I was going over the speed limit.' That will immediately give him a positive image instead of a negative one, and more times than not, he'll let you off with a warning rather than a ticket."

I listened and stored his advice in my brain for a time when I might try it. Not too long after that we were headed to Amelia Island for our annual two weeks of summer vacation. As soon as we got there, the children fled to the beach, and I laid down for my first nap of my vacation. Just as I dozed off, Denise ran into the house screaming, "Mama, come quick. Deanna has broken her leg." I thought they were playing a trick on me, so I just rolled over and tried to ignore the situation. Finally, when she kept after me, I realized that this was no joke. Deanna had indeed broken her ankle showing off on a disc board. She missed the board and somehow broke her ankle. We spent the first afternoon of our vacation at the hospital in Fernandina Beach. I tell you this only to preface the next part of the story.

Two weeks later our time at the beach was up and we had to leave. As usual, we came down in two cars, so we decided that since Deanna needed space for her leg—she was in a cast from her foot to her knee—Vince would bring everyone in the car and I would drive Deanna and all the luggage. My station wagon was loaded. Deanna and I decided to leave early Sunday morning while Vince and the others would stay a little longer.

I got up, put on shorts, a shirt, and flipflops, put on no makeup but lipstick, and pulled my hair back in a pony tail. I was in no mood to impress anyone. I just wanted to get Deanna home and to our orthopedic doctor, Butch Mulherin. Sunday mornings at the beach there is no traffic, and it was too early for even the churchgoers to be out on the road. The first little town after the Amelia bridge had a service station on the corner and a stop sign. You must understand, there is nobody on the road. So I saw the stop sign and almost stopped, but I didn't quite. I looked both ways and kind of rolled through it. Top speed was maybe one mile per hour.

No sooner had I rolled through it than out of the service station lot came blue lights right behind me. I was stunned; I really could not believe he was pulling me over. I pulled off on the side of the road and decided to do just what Vince had told me to do — get out of the car immediately and act humble. I put the car in park and turned the engine off and jumped out, shorts, shirt, flipflops and all. I immediately stuck out my hand to shake his and said, "Gosh, Officer, I am so sorry that I did not come to a complete stop."

He looked at me with cold, hard eyes and said, "Lady, get back in your car. Don't think you are going to proposition me with your body to get out of a ticket."

I almost died. I was so embarrassed and humiliated. Deanna began crying as I got into the car. Neither of us could believe what we had heard. First of all, I have never been known for my body, and secondly, he was the last person in the world I would ever think of giving my body to for a forty-five dollar ticket. He was insulting me! I was so taken aback that I was actually speechless, and that has only happened a few times in my life. Vince's advice was worthless. I drove off with a crying child, a deflated ego, and a ticket.

Our children were always noisy and loud. I never realized what the noise level was really like until they all left. No wonder I was a wreck. They not only talked loud, but they were always fighting and picking on each other. I thought that was the way everybody's children were, so most of the time I could overlook it. But ever so often, they would get on my nerves until I was a screaming basket case.

I was driving them all to Birmingham for a visit home right before Christmas, and Vince was to follow later. Derek was two and in a car seat next to me in the front seat, and the other three—ages ten, eight, and seven—were in the back seat raising Cain. They were fighting and arguing over who was in whose space. They didn't want to be touched, so they had imaginary lines that nobody could cross. We had a three-seater wagon, but with all the luggage, we couldn't use the way-back seat.

You must understand that this was before Interstate 20 was open, and the five-hour trip took us through one little town after another. Right about at the state line I had had enough. I was screaming at the children, and I had just reached around Derek and blasted one of them, whoever had been in my path. I was in a major fit when, without thinking, I rolled through a stop sign. Truly, I had no idea what I had done. I was so angry at the children that I was totally unaware of the world outside the car.

The blue lights came on, and now I really flipped. Not only did I not want to stop, but at that time in our life I could not afford a ticket. As the officer approached my car, I started sobbing uncontrollably. When I get really mad, I cry. The officer gently said, "Lady, let me see your driver's license." As I reached for it, the children were sitting perfectly straight and silent, and the fact that it took a policeman to shut them up made me even madder. The officer said, "Do you know what you did?"

For some reason that really set me off, and I began screaming at him and crying at the same time.

"Do I know what I did? Heck no, I don't know what I did. Have you ever tried to drive with four wild children who fight all the time? My nerves have had it."

"But lady," he said, "you could kill your whole family if you continue not to notice stop signs."

"Good," I said. "I am looking forward to seeing Jesus. It

beats the heck out of the hell that they are putting me through in this car."

"Now lady," he said soothingly, "you have got to calm down, and as for you children, look how upset you have gotten your mother." He then proceeded to give them a lecture on behavior. He knew they were scared, so he could make an impression. He ended by saying, "Now, you all follow me, and I'll buy you a treat, but I'll expect you to be good to your mother so she can drive you safely to your grandmother's house."

But here's the story I started out to tell. During the days Vince was considering running for governor, we spent most of our time in the car going to Atlanta to talk to people about strategy, and we always went together. But on this particular gray December Sunday, I really didn't want to go with him. I had, without realizing it, become his slave, his chauffeur, and I was fed up. I would drive, and he would work all the way to Atlanta. No conversation, no radio — just drive him there, and when he was ready, drive him home. I had things that I wanted to do at home, but when his mind is set on your doing something, you had better forget what you want to do.

I got behind the wheel, but not with a wonderful attitude. I drove him all the way to Atlanta as he dictated, and when he was ready to come home, I drove him back in silence. With every mile, I was getting madder and madder, and I was going faster and faster. Finally, when we got to Monroe, Georgia, he slowly pulled his glasses onto his forehead, looked at me with a cold glare, and said, "You had better slow down or you are going to get a ticket."

Well, that totally infuriated me, and, as my nature would have it, I accelerated. I was pushing ninety when I heard the policeman. As I was pulling off the road, Vince looked at me and said, "What did I tell you? I hope he slaps you with a big ticket."

I stopped the car, and Vince jumped out and said, "Officer, I just told her to slow down. I hope you write her the biggest ticket you have ever given." The policeman came to my window and asked for my license. I handed it to him without saying a word. He looked at it and looked at me. "I clocked you at eighty-seven miles per hour. Why in the world would you be going so fast?"

I looked him straight in the eye and said, "Have you ever been in a car with an SOB and you couldn't wait to get home?" He looked at me with a smirk. I am sure that was one response he had never heard.

"Barbara," he said, "I understand. Hit it and go on." Now that was an understanding policeman.

"YOU ONLY TURN FIFTY ONCE"

Birthdays have always been special in our house. In fact, birthdays were really the biggest holidays of all to me. There's something special about the day that each of us is born; it's the only day of the year that is truly ours and that doesn't have to be shared with anyone else in the family. Given my attitude, it's not surprising that all of our children grew up loving birthdays. It was their day. They could choose whatever they wanted to eat for each meal, and they really got to be the boss all day.

Unfortunately, it was a little different for Vince and me. Our birthdays fall in early September, which for a coach is the busiest time of year. Two-a-day practices are not conducive to happy birthdays, for either of us. He's never happy because it's football season and he is "focused," and I'm never happy because I don't feel like he really remembers. In fact, we finally had to make an agreement that the week before my birthday I would remind him, and that way I would not have to go into my annual depression from having my birthday forgotten.

I remember this one year I was dropping the news on him as he was reading the newspaper at the breakfast table. He has a way of reading the morning paper while I'm talking to him and answering me without really listening; he's just hearing. Anyway, I said to him, "Vincent, my birthday is next Monday."

He said, "Uh hunh."

"Vincent," I repeated, "my birthday is next Monday, and you told me to remind you."

"So what do you want?" he asked without ever moving the paper.

"I want a divorce," I said, just to make sure he wasn't really listening.

With his face still buried behind the paper, he calmly answered, "I wasn't planning on spending that much."

But there were some birthdays that will always be remembered, and those are the ones that I want to share with you.

I never thought about turning thirty until the day actually came. It might have been the most depressing birthday of my life because it made me feel that I was really grown up and I didn't like that feeling. After all, who in their right mind would want to leave their twenties — the years when you know everything about everything and have a carefree attitude about everything around you. Thirty just sounded so old. Why, I was still saying "yes ma'am" to forty-year-olds. Of course, Vince was gone by six o'clock that morning. I was still asleep. and he didn't wish me happy birthday, so I woke up feeling sorry for myself. My oldest child was eight, and she did a gallant job of getting the rest of the group to sing "Happy Birthday" at breakfast, but I knew that if there were to be a cake, I had to bake it. Somehow that takes the fun out of your own birthday.

I left the house that day with only one mission — to do whatever I wanted to do. After having lunch with friends, I went shopping to buy my own birthday present. I ended up with a black slinky nightgown. I thought my sex appeal was gone, and now I needed a costume. Vince never realized how hard I was taking the day until he came home for dinner with a sportswriter friend. Back then coaches did have sportswriters as friends. I had fixed my usual Tuesday night fare — meatloaf — and one of our coaches' wives had baked me a cake after all. We had my little party with all the children blowing out the candles and singing, but there were no presents. Vincent had forgotten. I went to my room and fell apart. I couldn't believe that he would forget this day, but I couldn't make a scene because we had company and I didn't want the children to see me. Tuesday night was my bridge night, so I composed myself, cleaned the kitchen, got the baby-sitter, kissed the children goodbye (Vince having already gone back to work by this time), and left for the evening. When I returned, there on the kitchen table was Dean Martin's hit record album EVERYBODY LOVES SOMEBODY SOMETIME. He had come through again, late in the fourth quarter. How can you stay mad with a gift like that?

Vince had a sense of humor that I didn't always appreciate on my birthdays. I was used to being "queen for a day" when growing up, and that was what I still wanted and expected. For some reason, Vince wanted to make me wait, get me upset, and then give me my present. Even the first year of our marriage, my birthday came and not one word was said about it. Vince went to work and still nothing. He came home for dinner and nothing. I tried to be calm. I tried to be silent, but I was getting madder and madder and he knew it.

Finally, at 11:45 p.m., as we were going to bed and my birthday was almost over, I cracked and pitched a fit about how unthoughtful he was and how he had ruined my day. He laughed and said, "It's not over yet." I said, "As far as I'm concerned, it is."

While I started crying, he reached under the bed and pulled out a huge box. At this point, I didn't even want it, but he convinced me to open it. It was a beautiful dress, but as far as I was concerned, he had ruined my special day. I think he realized that he had carried his little joke too far.

Years later, when he knew he was going to be out of town on my birthday, he got the children together and they had a surprise plan. He would come home on Friday night, September 7, and have to leave early on September 8. He told them to go to bed and he would wake them, and we would have a party at midnight to celebrate my birthday. I couldn't understand why I didn't have a problem getting the children to bed by nine o'clock on a Friday night. They went down like angels. I went to bed about ten and at 12:01 was waked up by Vince and the children singing "Happy Birthday" and bearing a cake and gifts. It was a real surprise and one of the best birthdays I can remember.

I'm not sure that I ever dreaded reaching forty because my thirties were so awful, but I knew I didn't want a silly "forty" celebration. "Lordy, Lordy, Barbara is forty" was a phrase that gagged me every time I heard it, and I made it clear that I didn't want any fanfare. When Vince turned forty, I gave him a party at the school cafeteria because I knew that I wouldn't be able to get him home. So we celebrated with all the coaches and their wives after dinner at the football dorm, and he went straight back to the office after his last bite of cake.

The unfortunate thing about my fortieth was that we were a week late opening the season that year, and my birthday fell on the Saturday that kicked off the football schedule. I knew what Vince would be doing—practicing football that morning and then watching the Alabama game on television that night. I had no fear that he would remember my birthday, though I had told him emphatically that I didn't want any kind of a party. I just wanted to be left alone. I had planned on taking our two girls to Atlanta for the day. We would shop and have lunch, which would be the best birthday I could think of. We had invited our long-time friends Bill and Ruth Hartman over for dinner, and we were just going to be quiet and watch football. It really wasn't my style, but it was what I thought I wanted.

Of course, what I wanted was irrelevant anyway. If I expect something, I don't get it. If I don't expect anything, I get it all. And did I ever get it all on this day.

Vince had called Hugh Christian at WRFC, one of the local radio stations that carried our games, and persuaded him to have a "Guess Who's Going To Be Forty" contest on the radio. Every day they would give a clue and have a daily winner, and at the end of the week, on my birthday, they would draw from the daily winners and get a grand prize winner. The winner would get two tickets for the opening football game on the forty-yard line. I never heard the clues, nor did I know anything at all about the contest, but I did think it odd that strange people would come up to me and ask if my birthday was Saturday. I would smile and politely say yes, never really wondering about how they knew.

Finally, Saturday morning, my birthday morning, our housekeeper came to work and said, "Mrs. Dooley, is today your birthday?"

"Yes," I said. "How did you know?"

"I knew it was you, I just knew it was you," she started screaming. "I should have called and I could have won, 'cause I just knew it was you."

"What are you talking about?" I asked.

"You know," she said, "on the radio, they is giving your clues."

"I don't understand what you are talking about," I said.

"Turn on the radio and you'll hear," she said.

I did and I heard all I needed to hear. He had really done it to me this time. There were no "Lordy, Lordy, Barbara is forty" signs; instead, all of the city knew I was forty. But that was only the beginning of the best decade of my life. I woke that morning to Vince's arm around me — a real shocker since it was Saturday, the first day of football season, and thoughts of anything but football were rare. It was seven o'clock in the morning, and by all rights he should have been at the office. Not only was he not getting up to go to the office, but he wanted to stay in bed and talk. Now that should have been a dead giveaway that something was about to happen. The last time that he wanted to talk, Kennedy was our president. He was rattling on and on to keep me in bed when finally, on our back patio, I heard the Georgia Band, led by our team chaplain and longtime friend Claude McBride, playing "The Georgia Fight Song" and then "Happy Birthday." Vince picked me up — tattered nightgown, unbrushed hair, unbrushed teeth — and carried me out the door and to present me to the group as his forty-year-old bride. I could have died. If only I had brushed my teeth!

They played music, held up banners, and everyone sang "Happy Birthday." The children thought this was the greatest thing their father had ever concocted. I had really been surprised, and it started my day off great. I thought, "This was painless, it was funny, and now it's over I can go to Atlanta and enjoy the day with my girls." Never in my wildest dreams did I think there would be more. Don't ever underestimate Vince Dooley.

We came home from Atlanta, and I was exhausted. I took my nice clothes off and put on grubs. Since we were staying home and watching football with the Hartmans, I just wanted to be comfortable. I was on the floor in front of the TV when I heard the Georgia Band. Sometimes on a real clear day we can hear the band practicing, and I thought how loud and clear it was. Then Derek ran in the back den and started screaming, "Mama, come quick. The band is marching down the street." I jumped up and ran outside with him, and there was my family with Vince cheering them on, laughing.

I looked up the drive, and there was the whole band, not just a few members, and behind them was a parade of people carrying signs and banners. These were not just ordinary people; they were my mother, brothers, sister, aunt, college roommate, and close friends, and they were all dressed in my clothes. They had come over while I was in Atlanta and robbed me of wigs, jewelry, housecoats, and dresses. All the women had something on of mine, all the men were wearing Vince's clothes, and they were having a parade down our street. At the end of the parade was a catering truck with food for the party. In one instant everyone I loved had appeared to wish me a happy birthday, and Vince had pulled off the biggest surprise of my life. I'm not sure that one can ever be equaled.

Later that evening as I opened my gifts, I was surprised by one of the most treasured gifts I've ever received from Vincent—a framed cross-stitch that said, "I love you more than football." I knew he really didn't mean it, but sometimes it's nice just hearing what you want to hear.

I was determined to do something really special for Vince's fiftieth, but I knew that I couldn't get him off the practice field to pull anything off. So I decided to take the party to practice. It was 1982, and we were in the glory years of Georgia football, but that still didn't make his personality pleasant during football season. He didn't smile until it was over and he knew the results.

I hired a belly dancer to meet me on the lower end of the field where the band practices. I talked with Roger Dancz, who was the band director, and he was going to let the belly dancer hide among the band members as the band marched onto the practice field. Then the belly dancer would show herself when they got in front of Vince. The plan sounded great, and I went to the practice field with great anticipation. I couldn't let Vince see me or he would know I was up to something, so I hid myself to watch the show. The band started marching across the practice field, which they had never been on during actual practice before, and I could see a puzzled look on Vince's face, like "What in the hell do they think they're doing?"

But they never wavered, just kept marching as the football players moved out of their way. They got in front of Vince and split in half, and out came the belly dancer. She turned on her tape player to start the music and began her gyrations. Vince was holding a whistle in his hand and he began twirling it around and around on its string. The players were going crazy. The closer the dancer got to Vince, the faster he twirled the whistle. Finally, when she was through, he looked at the team and said, "Men, if you had moves like this we could be undefeated." He then looked at me and said, "I'll see you when I get home after you practice your moves."

Fifty was fun when it was Vincent but I certainly wasn't looking forward to it. I loved the forty decade, and I was in no hurry for it to pass. All good things must come to an end, but the thought of ending that great era was miserable to me. As with my fortieth, I announced that I didn't want a birthday party. This time I meant it. I had planned on leaving town so that none of my friends would get into mischief with Vince and do me in again, but after talking with Deanna I decided to stay and face the music. You can't run away from your special day.

I was still insistent that there was to be no party, and all of my family and friends knew I was serious. I had it all planned. Vince was leaving town for an ESPN assignment on Thursday and would be gone the whole weekend. My birthday was on Friday, and I would ease into it alone. The perfect plan, but it was not to be. On Wednesday, the week before my birthday, Marianne Rogers' secretary called and informed me that Marianne was in Los Angeles but was planning on giving me a birthday luncheon and she wanted a guest list. I told her that I really didn't want a party, but she said that Marianne was giving it whether I wanted it or not, and I'd better give her a guest list or she would invent one. I knew that I had been one-upped.

I consented to a luncheon and gave her a guest list, but I could hardly sleep for worrying about a fiftieth birthday party. I really didn't want it. The next morning, as I was exercising, I thought, "Why not? Why not have a party and make it the best that anyone has ever gone to." I began to get excited as my imagination took over. I knew that if

Marianne were having a luncheon, every lady there would be dressed to the nines; they would wear the best they had and look prettier than ever. I would go the opposite way. I would dress up as an old woman and bring gifts to everybody who was invited. Ah, the idea was getting better. Now I was going to have fun, 'cause I was in control of my destiny. I called one of my closest friends, Ann Cabaniss, and told her my plan. I needed her help gathering my outfit and getting my makeup on.

Then I began planning my part on the program. I didn't want any mushy speeches or any nice accolades. I just wanted a fun birthday party. The big day arrived, and I started in on my makeup. I am olive-complected, so I put a white base on to make me look ancient. I used no eye makeup and no blush, just a lot of powder. Then I sprinkled baby powder all over my hair, and after I had the gray effect that I wanted, I pulled it all back in a knot on the back of my head. Ann had found me a little green hat with red cherries and a veil, and I plopped it on top of the bun. I had an old green dress with a white lace collar, white hose that I turned down at the ankles, my aunt Barbara's old fur skins that have the mink eyes staring at you, a pair of gold-rim glasses, white gloves, and the oldest, ugliest pocketbook that we could find. My shoes were vintage black skins, and all was perfect except that I needed some varicose veins in my legs. I had had mine operated on several years before, and now for one moment in time I needed them back. Ann took a blue magic marker and painted my legs. I picked up a cane, and my outfit was complete. I looked at least a hundred years old.

The perfect plan was unfolding. We called the Jennings Mill Country Club and told them that we had an elderly lady who needed some assistance and asked for someone

212

to escort her in. They assured us that they could accommodate us. I loaded the car with my gags and two cases of champagne, ready for a fun afternoon.

When we arrived, my escort was waiting for me and ushered me into the private room where the party was being held. I walked through the main dining room, and people that I had known for years did not recognize me. I knew that I had pulled it off. He opened the door to the private room, and all of my favorite friends were looking at me. For about ten seconds no one said anything, and I know they were thinking, "Who in the world is this bag lady?" All of a sudden Deanna screamed, "Mother." With that, everyone in the room got totally hysterical, and I knew that we were going to have a great party.

After lunch, Marianne stood and began a little speech about birthdays and turning fifty. I immediately interrupted and declared that I had something to say. I began in the softest, squeakiest voice I could find, a voice that I thought sounded really old. I said, "Last night as I was thinking about passing from one decade to another, I decided to throw away the things that I wouldn't need anymore so I brought them to you."

I reached down and pulled out the brown paper grocery sack I had been carrying, and I started pulling things out. First was a tube of toothpaste, and I said, "I won't need this anymore; now all I need is denture cream." Then I reached in and pulled out a bottle of hair color and said, "I don't think I'll ever need this stuff again because my hair is so gray it just won't wash in." My next item for show and tell was a pair of foam rubber, flesh-colored falsies. They really looked real and awful. I threw them on the table and said, "I sure don't need these anymore. I hang so low that these would tickle my kneecaps."

By this point everyone was in disbelief, and my daughter was horrified. But I wasn't through yet, by any means. I reached down in my bag and pulled out a package of birth control pills. I threw them on the table and said, "I sure don't need these anymore. The only thing I'm trying to control now is my bladder." Finally, with my friends' faces registering total shock, I reached in and pulled out a box of condoms.

Before I finish this tale, I must tell you how I bought them. I had never in my fifty years ever seen a condom, and I sure had not bought one. I was a little timid about it, but I got my nerve up and went into Hodgson's, a drug store we have been trading with for twenty-seven years and said, "I would like a box of condoms." Mac, the pharmacist, looked at me and started laughing and said, "What in the world do you want a box of condoms for?" I said, "Just don't ask questions and sell me a box of condoms. I'll explain later." I didn't know if they came in sizes or not, so I added, "And give me the biggest ones you have." Mac said, "I don't know what you're going to do, but I'm sure you're going to have a great time doing it." I told him that I didn't need any of his cute remarks, and I left with condoms in hand, charged to Vince Dooley's account.

Before the waiter had escorted me into the club, I had showed him two cases of champagne that I wanted passed out at the appropriate time. He was to put them out of sight until I gave him the word. As I pulled the condoms out of the box, my friends were laughing so hard that some were crying and others were screeching. I gave each one of them a condom and told the waiter to pass out the champagne. When they each had both, I said, "This is my final gift to you." I opened the condom and began stretching and pulling on it, and then I said, "I sure don't need this anymore 'cause it's obvious I don't know what to do with them. Now I want all of you to go home and give your husbands the champagne and the condom, toast me, and have a super evening." It was a great way to start a new decade.

Later that afternoon I got a call from one of my friends' husbands. He said, "I've never in my life sent my wife to a ladies' birthday luncheon where the favors were champagne and condoms. But then Barbara Dooley turns fifty only once!"

"BARBARA WHO?"

People often ask, "How have you stayed married so long? What is your secret?" There's really no secret. It's just that it's no longer fashionable to have unconditional love. It's no longer fashionable to be taken for granted, but that's what people who stay married so long do. They take each other's love for granted, they build on that love, and they continue to love each other no matter what the circumstances. Most schools love their football coaches. They love their basketball coaches. They just love their coaches — if their coaches are winning. The old saying among alumni is, "I'll love you win or tie." That is conditional love. But the saying of most football coaches' wives is, "I love you whether you win or lose." Love is commitment, and when you marry a football coach, you are making a supreme commitment.

When we first got married, in the early sixties, it was rare to hear of a football coach getting divorced. It was almost a divorce-free profession. But through the years I have watched it change; I have seen the effects of the growing feminist attitude toward marriage. Today's woman is not putting up with what it takes to be a dedicated football coach. She's not putting up with the idea of not sharing household jobs and not sharing in the raising of the children and not sharing in every facet of life. I'm sure this is at least partly because most coaches' wives are now working and are no longer defined by the single role of wife and homemaker. Now both partners are working, and so the roles have to be shared. When coaches' wives get together from all over the country, we share our problems, we laugh a lot, we discuss our lives, and one of the things we talk about is how fleeting love is in the business we're in and how it hurts us to know that people love us so conditionally. If our husband wins, we're accepted. If our husband doesn't win, we're rejected. And I think this is so true with our children. If their parents are doing well, they're accepted. If their parents are not doing well, they're rejected. This kind of love makes for a very unstable, unsatisfying condition. And the only way to keep your children grounded is to give them unconditional love and let them understand from the beginning about human nature.

I had four children by the time I was thirty. I had a husband who worked all the time, and I had an attitude problem. I didn't understand what I was supposed to get out of my life. In my opinion, it certainly wasn't staying at home, raising children, and never doing anything as a couple. On a day-to-day basis, there were very few moments that Vince and I spent together getting to know each other, just talking about who we were and how we felt about things. I was married to a man who couldn't take me for a ride on Sunday afternoon because he was watching films, who couldn't be with me on Friday night because he was at a high school game, who couldn't be with me on Saturday because he was coaching. I was being deprived, I was miserable, and I had a bad attitude.

It wasn't until I was in my mid-thirties that I finally looked around and thought, "Nobody is responsible for your happiness but you." All these years I had been making my husband responsible for my happiness, but he can't bring it to me. I had been making my children responsible for my happiness, but they can't bring it to me. I finally realized that happiness is something that comes from within; it's self-worth, it's self-esteem, it's purpose.

I would tell Vince how unhappy and miserable I was, and he would say he couldn't understand that. He wasn't miserable, and he wasn't unhappy.

"Yeah," I would tell him, "I can see why you are happy. You get dressed, you go to work every day, and everybody tells you how wonderful you are. Nobody tells me how wonderful I am. Nobody tells me how nice I look or what a great job I'm doing. No wonder you've got a great life. You get reinforcement all the time, plus you get a feeling of accomplishment."

When we first came to Georgia, I was almost paranoid about people liking me only because my husband was the head coach. This feeling stayed with me for years. Every time someone tried to become my friend, I thought, "Would this person want to be my friend if Vince weren't the head coach?" And more times than not the answer was "no." I never had a problem making friends in grammar school, high school, or college. It was only when I got married and had this identity defined by who my husband was that I became very insecure about my relationships with other people. In fact, I'm not sure that I trusted any friendship for years.

Vince constantly reminded me how fleeting our job security was and told me to always be ready to move, and this mentality did its number on me. It took me years of prayer and reading to realize that his job did open many doors, but to keep them open was my responsibility. That's what we tried to teach our children, that many times people would either do them favors because of their dad or do them harm because of their dad, but, regardless, they were individuals and whatever they did ultimately reflected on them.

People don't always realize how they affect you, but attitudes come through; love comes through and so does hypocrisy. I've been introduced to people with the line, "This is Barbara Dooley," and they've said, "Oh, how are you" in a perfectly natural way. Then, after a couple of sentences, they realize that Vince Dooley is my husband, and their whole personality changes. They immediately get a glow in their eye, they want to be my best friend, and they never leave me the rest of the evening. They don't realize how obvious it is that it wasn't for Barbara Dooley that they wanted to be my friend, but for Vince Dooley. Football coaches are celebrities, plain and simple. Everyone knows them and has formed judgments about them. Very few people actually know the coach's wife, but they are quick to judge her according to her husband's accomplishments. This was so clear to me not long ago when Vince was thinking about running for governor. One morning as we were driving to Atlanta, which is about an hour-and-a-half drive, to catch a flight to New York, one of our local talk-show hosts, Ludlow Porch, had as his topic for the day, "If Vince Dooley ran for governor, would you vote for him?"

At first I was excited about listening to what people had to say, and then I got a little nervous about the possibility of a bad phone call and what it would do to Vince to hear somebody say something negative about him. As we began listening, all of the calls that came in were very favorable. Everybody was talking about how much they loved Vince Dooley, how much they respected him, how smart he was, what a wonderful coach he was and Vince never showed any sign of emotion during the whole program. I thought I noticed his head getting bigger and bigger, but I wasn't positive. I was absorbing every bit of it and wondering just when that negative caller was going to call because inevitably it had to happen.

Sure enough, about an hour into the program a call came through from a lady who identified herself as "Silver Britches" from Gainesville, Georgia. Ludlow, in his own good-buddy way, welcomed her to the show, told her he hadn't heard from her in a long time, and was glad that she had called. And then he said, "Well, Silver Britches, if Vince Dooley ran for governor, would you vote for him?"

Without the slightest hesitation, she said, "No, I would not vote for Vince Dooley. I hate Vince Dooley."

Noting the force behind her voice, Ludlow said, "Silver Britches, why in this world would you hate Vince Dooley?"

Again she answered immediately: "I hate the University of Georgia, and I would never vote for anyone from the University of Georgia."

Ludlow calmly told her that that was no way to pick a governor. "You've got to have a better reason than that," he said. "I'm going to give you ten seconds to think about it and then we'll come back on the air and ask you why you wouldn't vote for Vince Dooley for governor."

Ten seconds doesn't seem like a long time, but ten seconds of dead air on the radio is a long time, especially when you are waiting for an answer like that. Finally, she came back on, and Ludlow said, "Okay, Silver Britches, now that you've had a little time to think about it, why wouldn't you vote for Vince Dooley for governor?"

She said, "Well, Ludlow, to be perfectly honest, I couldn't stand four years of Baa-Bra." Silver Britches obviously didn't like my drawl, which, of course, was the only thing she knew about me.

At that point I almost fell out of the car. Vince and I were both cracking up, and Ludlow said, "You don't even know Barbara."

Silver Britches said, "I know but I can't stand her anyway."

Vince calmly looked at me and said, "You see, they know what a saint I am to live with Baa-Bra."

So many of us say that we can't stand people when we don't even know them. I honestly believe that we can love anybody we get to know, but the trouble with us today is that we don't take the time to know our neighbor. In fact, we don't even take the time to know our spouse or our children. We go through our days just to get through them; we're not really alive.

As long as you feel that you're not being loved for yourself and for what you are but what your husband is and what he's done, you can't develop a healthy self-image. This is a problem for so many wives, and it will stay a problem until we resolve within ourselves that we are people, too, loving and lovable people, and worthy on our own merits. But before we come to this conclusion, many of us have to go through a long period of suffering, and that's what I did. I went through a period of watching my husband outgrow me, of watching him work very hard get lots of credit and adulation, while I stood still. You can imagine the feelings that were silently growing inside me — the bitterness, envy, and self-doubt. As Barry Switzer's ex-wife so aptly put it, after he was so successful so soon, "It's tough living with God."

The thing is, we made a commitment to love each other when we got married, but that love had to grow. Each of us changes personalities; we don't remain the same, and we shouldn't. Each decade — each year — we grow and change, so after we've been married thirty years or forty years, we're not the same two people who married at the age of twenty. The key is to grow together, with both partners developing their sense of personality or style and yet supporting the other. And this is where I tended to get lost in my thirties. I let myself be overwhelmed by his success and had so little of my own. I was raising a family. I was riding his coattails, and I saw very little worthwhile in myself. This negative attitude permeated my being. I just spiraled downward until I realized that I was becoming something that I really detested. I had always been a loving, trusting person, and I found myself fearing to love because I didn't know if others really loved me or my husband.

Cardinal Newman, the noted British theologian, once said, "Fear not that your life will have an end, or that you're going to die, but fear that your life will never have a beginning." Of course, taking charge of your life and honestly trying to make positive changes is not that easy. It has to be a constant effort, but if you are dedicated to really trying, it almost consumes you. It's something like going on a diet; once you begin to see results, it's full steam ahead.

The first thing I did was try to approach my life as a profession. I began getting up every morning before anyone else, showering, fixing my hair, putting on makeup, and wearing nice casual clothes. For years I had gotten up, put on my robe, brushed my teeth, and given my hair a quick brush-through, and sometimes I wouldn't actually get dressed until mid-morning. Even then I would just put on grub clothes to clean the house. That was coming to a halt. It did take effort, but the response from the whole family was amazing. The children had better attitudes at breakfast, and at first Vince would ask, "Where are you going so early?" But after awhile they came to expect a fresh face at breakfast.

So many of us who don't work out of the home keep our robe on most of the day. When I look back on those years, I realize that Vince would leave for work and see me in a robe and then would come home late at night and see me in the same robe. Not only that, it was the same robe day after day, month after month, year after year. That was another tactic — buy more robes. At least when I wore one, I could make it fresh and pretty.

At first it was weird to clean the toilets in nice clothes, but after awhile it honestly made housework seem bearable. It's funny how your family comes to expect certain things from you, and it's scary how your children see you as a standard when they are young. A few years after I had implemented my new philosophy on housekeeping, Deanna spent the night out with a friend. She came home and said, "Mama, can you believe her mother comes to the table in her robe?"

When we first came to Athens, I had taught public speaking at the university and had loved it. I knew that I didn't have time to teach again, but I wanted to do something that would give me the feeling of accomplishment. I was asked to introduce Vince at a banquet here in Athens, and I accepted. I worked long and hard so as to be able to offer a unique introduction, and I was successful. The audience laughed and clapped, and the main speaker, Red Mitchum, looked at me and said, "Lady, you ought to go on the road. You're a good speaker."

I thanked him and really thought no more about it until people started calling and asking me to speak to their groups. I accepted every invitation, and I loved it. For the first time in a long time, I was feeling that I was doing something. After every speech, I would come home with a flower, or a box of candy, or a trinket from the group's members. That was nice, but then I would see Vince come home from his speaking engagements with a check.

"Something is wrong," I said. "I'm just as good a speaker as you are, but no one is paying me; all I get is some sort of token."

"Well," Vince said, "start charging."

That was something I almost couldn't do. I had never talked money with anybody. Why, no Southern lady would do that. But I was determined that I had gotten my last potted plant for speaking. When the next call came asking me to speak to a group, I very weakly said, "I have to apologize, but I have to charge."

"That's fine," said the caller. "What is your fee?"

Of course, I hadn't really thought that far, and for a moment I couldn't answer. Then I said, "Exactly what you pay my husband."

Now I was on my way to regaining my own individuality, and everything around me took on new meaning. I had close friends who I knew loved me whether we won or lost or whether I was married to Vince Dooley or not, and those "fringe friends" I was able to handle a lot better. I was finally getting my life back in control. I was rebuilding the self-esteem I felt I had sacrificed to Vince's all-encompassing job. I was starting to live, and that felt good.

I would not be telling the truth if I did not tell you how much I prayed. I honestly laid my life, my whole being, in the hands of Jesus and begged Him to help me, to help my marriage and to help our children overcome this problem. A Christian marriage is based on Jesus's unconditional love and until we accept that, it's hard for us to be able to give love to others. I had always been opinionated, but had tried to keep my thoughts to myself if I thought it might interfere with Vince's job. But now I stepped out on my own, going to prayer groups, and having them at our home. I didn't care what people said about me; I believed this way and I was going to live the way I believed.

As I look back, it truly amazes me how one can turn his life around with a concerted effort. Sports gives any coaching family a false sense of love and security. When you win, everyone loves you, and you feel secure and warm. When you lose, it's the exact opposite. This is a perfect example of conditional, and it's exactly what we don't want to impart to our children. We want our husbands, our spouses, our children to know that we love unconditionally. It doesn't matter what they do or how they act, we will love them.

But sports doesn't lend itself to this attitude, so it's a hard thing to teach children in a sports-oriented family.

For that matter, it's a hard thing to teach children under any circumstances, given the social milieu we live in today. The astronomical divorce rate is proof enough that today's children don't have any sense of unconditional love. "For better or for worse, for richer or for poorer, till death do us part" are the words most of us say when we get married. But when things get bad, we forget all that; we forget the unconditional love that we pledged to each other. We change the words to "You haven't met my conditions, you haven't done this or that, so I'm gone."

This is a frightening thing for children. It's frightening to see their daddy's job on the line because of a win or loss column. It's frightening for children to wake up and think that their parents, who committed to love, are all of a sudden out of love and divorced. What's to keep the child from thinking, if they can fall out of love with each other, they might fall out of love with me. That's a scary thought for a child, and that's why it's so important for families to unite and show unconditional love. To show our children that no matter what the disagreements, no matter what the win or loss record, no matter what comes in life, we pledge ourselves to each other, we're growing together, we're loving together, and we're fighting all obstacles together.

That is what love and family and commitment truly mean. It is not conveniently getting rid of a person because he or she doesn't think like we think. It's not conveniently throwing out a friendship because of one bad word or bad idea. It's not like taking a piece of clothing out of your closet and updating. You don't update friendships; you add to friendships. You don't update or add spouses; you grow together in a deeper commitment.

Marriage is a lot like football, in that it takes a lot of work every single day, and in that it teaches the value of teamwork. Individuality is great, but working together for the team is better. And that's what we do in families; we encourage everyone's individuality, but we want to work together as a team. I can remember in 1980, our national championship year, our coaches had t-shirts printed up for our whole team to wear. In big, twelve-inch letters was the word "TEAM," and right underneath in one-inch letters was the word "ME." Big "TEAM" and little "ME."

That year of the championship, our team had a special bond that not many teams have. It was a unique group of guys who will be friends; no matter what their background, no matter where they go, they will have a closeness of spirit that will never be captured again. That's what we see when we look at some families and we say, "Gosh, what a neat family. They seem to be so happy." What we are looking at is a team. Maybe the husband is the head coach of the family and the wife is the assistant head coach who directs everything. In the final analysis, someone has to be head of the household, and while husband and wife are equal, in our family you could say Vince is first among equals. Everyone knows his position and everyone pitches in to play his position well.

Unlike a football team, the family's players don't graduate every year, so we have many years to develop a winning team. We have many years to build that solid love relationship, and I'm not sure that we're ever really finished. As the children get older and get married, our love just extends to their spouses and their children, and the team can only get better and deeper. "For better or for worse, for richer or for poorer" — the pledge of unconditional love binds the family through the generations.